Entertaining with Insects

Or: The Original Guide To Insect Cookery

Ronald L. Taylor*
Barbara J. Carter

*Author of Butterflies in My Stomach: or, Insects in Human Nutrition

Illustrated by John Gregory Tweed

Published by
WOODBRIDGE PRESS PUBLISHING COMPANY
Santa Barbara, California 93111

Published by

Woodbridge Press Publishing Company
Post Office Box 6189
Santa Barbara, California 93111

Library of Congress Catalog Card Number: 76-47163

International Standard Book Number: 0-912800-37-2

Published simultaneously in the United States and Canada

Printed in the United States of America

Life cycle drawings by Kathryn Bill.

Dedication

To our adventurous friends.

Acknowledgements

We are grateful to our good friends—
Bonnie Bair, Mike Riley, Bob Hodges, and John
Gregory Tweed—for their editorial assistance and
helpful suggestions regarding the organization of
this book.

We also wish to express our thanks to Fred
Rhyme of the Rainbow Bait Co., Compton,
California, for his kindness in providing
us with the mealworms used to develop
our recipes, to Mike Young of the Bait Barn
Worm Farm, Coeur d'Alene, Idaho, for supplying
us with earthworms, and to J. Manke, Alhambra,
California, for providing us with honey bees.

Contents

Introduction

Introduction

A visit to any large bookstore will probably leave one with the idea that there are too many cookbooks already, so why add to the list? In this case, however, the addition to the mountains of gastronomical know-how is different enough to be unique. You are thumbing through the first book of insect cookery ever to be printed. Most people have never thought of cooking insects. As a matter of fact, most people shudder at the thought, and this is unfortunate. Insects, in general, are wholesome and nutritious, and they can be delicious!

This cookbook, which is intended to be informative and fun, is the outgrowth of an earlier book by one of the present authors, Ronald L. Taylor, entitled *Butterflies in My Stomach or Insects in Human Nutrition* (Woodbridge Press, Santa Barbara). That work's scope and intention are broader and, in a sense, more serious. Briefly summarized, it shows that numerous insects are cleaner than many of the animals man regularly eats, there are no special religious prohibitions against the eating of insects as such, insects have been eaten throughout man's history and are eaten today, certain insects are relished and regarded as delicacies by civilized as well as primitive societies, insects are likely to be the most reliable source of animal food for the individual lost in the wilderness, insects play significant roles as therapeutic agents in man's drug arsenal, and, perhaps most important, insects are clearly a nutritious source of human food. As the book makes clear, insect eating (entomophagy) is not inherently abhorrent or unnatural—in fact, quite the contrary—for insects are a perfectly acceptable alternative source of food for man.

This is an important fact in view of the present and predicted world food dilemma, for we are being forced to reexamine basic concepts of human nutrition and to search for simple, inexpensive, and nutritious food. The development of such food should be a matter of primary concern to all of us, for if the human race is to survive, we cannot afford to leave unexplored the world's still unknown food potential. In a time of increasing food shortages and protein deficiency worldwide, the possibilities of incorporating insects into our diets merit serious consideration and research.

In our experience we have discovered that if people can overcome their prejudices and try insect dishes, they usually like them very much. As we more and more often saw this to be the case, we were drawn to the idea of an insect cookbook, for it seems an ideal way to demonstrate the point while at the same time providing an original way to feed and entertain your guests and your family. Practical insect recipes, however, are hard to come by. In researching *Butterflies in My Stomach,* significant sources such as the staff of *Gourmet Magazine* and *Foods of the World* (Time-Life Books) were contacted and were unable to locate a single insect recipe. When we began the cookbook, then, it was clear that we would have to develop the recipes ourselves.

In many of our recipes the insect is unrecognizable. In fact, in most cases if a person hasn't been told that insects are a part of the dish, he will be completely unaware. This of course, is not to advocate "tricking" your guests. Rather, it simply emphasizes that objections to eating insects have little or nothing to do with their taste or food value. If there is a problem, it arises from what we bring to the insect rather than what the insect brings to us.

In preparing this cookbook we have tested a number of insects and a wide variety of ways of preparing them. We have also contacted numerous commercial insect dealers. The names and addresses of those who responded to our inquiries and who were able to provide useful insects and information are included in the appropriate appendices. Doubtless there are dealers we have overlooked, and we would be pleased to hear from them. This is particularly important because the commercial availability of an insect was one of our principal considerations in the choice of insects for our recipes. For this reason all our recipes center around the mealworm (a beetle larva), the cricket, and the honey bee. The only unfortunate aspect of this is that it has meant that we've had to exclude some insects that are particularly tasty—in some cases even tastier than those we have included.

Our recipes range from breads (where the insect is ground up and added to flour) to minestrone (where the insect is intact). We have divided the book into five sections which contain complete menus to assist you in your meal planning. In order to round out some of our menus, we have added a few dishes which do not incorporate insects.

These are fairly common dishes, and for that reason we have not provided recipes for them. For the benefit of those who may only be interested in a particular dish, there is a recipe index. In addition there is a section entitled "Basics," containing information on such things as the preparation of marinades and broths and the dry roasting of insects, which is applicable throughout the book. The appendices contain information on obtaining insects, cleaning and preparing them for cooking, and a special section on earthworm cookery. About the latter a word needs to be said, for earthworms are not classified scientifically as insects. Indeed, many of the creatures which people customarily refer to as insects are not properly so designated. Insects, strictly speaking, belong to the major animal group known as arthropods, which have "skeletons" on the outside of their bodies, and have jointed walking legs—three pairs in the case of insects. Earthworms, of course, are legless. Nonetheless, because of current interest in their use as human food, we have decided to include them.

As this introductory discussion makes clear, the subject of insects as human food is a large and complicated one. Here, though, we are more interested in its amusing and entertaining aspects. Thus, we have enjoyed preparing this book, experimenting with recipes and insects, and we hope you will find among its pages many new dishes and an adventure in food and entertainment.
Bon Appétit!

The Cocktail Party

We are told that Gertrude Stein and Alice B. Toklas invented the cocktail party shortly after the turn of the century in a joint fit of desperation. They had too many friends and acquaintances and just couldn't imagine how they could entertain them in herds aside from simply slaking their thirst and then sending them out, thus fortified, to dine. At first this was an idea that was greeted with universal admiration. Today, decades later, the cocktail party is not only old hat, it generally is a crashing bore, *pro forma*, and usually obligatory ("I know it'll be ghastly, dear, but they'll *kill* us if we don't go.") Guests seldom find anything to talk about anymore except each other and the host's inferior hors d'ouevres, so we have come up with an idea that we think Gertrude and especially Alice would have liked, if not positively relished. *Serve insects!* No more boredom. No more gossip. No lack of things to discuss. Let our six-legged friends become the life of the party with the suggested recipes that follow.

Menu

Jalapa Dip

Ron's Favorite Mushrooms

Stuffed Cherry Tomatoes

Petula Clark Canapés

Cricket Rumaki   Tillamook Tarts

Salted Garlic Mealworms

Cricket Crisps

Bacon=Pepper Bees

Jalapa Dip

From Jalapa, Guatemala, comes the idea for this spicy dip.

½ cup Basic Cooked Insects, chopped
 (see *Basics*)
½ cup cottage cheese
3 tablespoons jalapeño peppers
2 tablespoons chives, chopped
2 tablespoons cilantro, minced
2 teaspoons lemon juice
1 teaspoon cumin
Salt and pepper to taste

Combine all ingredients. Mix well and chill. Serve with crudités such as jicama and celery.

Ron's Favorite Mushrooms

Since Ron loves cream cheese and mushrooms, we decided to put them together. Here's what we came up with.

2 dozen cleaned mushrooms
 (approximately 1½ inches in diameter)
1 package (8-ounce) cream cheese
½ cup Basic Cooked Insects, minced
 (see *Basics*)
1 tablespoon fresh dill, minced

Remove the mushroom stems from caps and save for other recipes. Mix cream cheese, minced dill, and minced insects. Stuff mushroom caps* with the mixture and place on a cookie sheet or shallow baking dish; broil until browned. Serve while still warm.

*Sautéed Mushrooms (see *Basics*) may be used if desired.

Stuffed Cherry Tomatoes

Candied insects are a delightful garnish, as you will discover with this recipe.

Cherry tomatoes
1 package (8-ounce) cream cheese
2 tablespoons onion, grated
Candied Insects (crickets or bees) (see *Basics*)

Combine cream cheese and onion. Remove center of tomatoes and stuff with cream cheese mixture. Top with a candied cricket or bee.

Petula Clark Canapés

When Ron appeared on the Mike Douglas Show, he was asked to prepare a French dish for Petula Clark. We prepared this canapé especially for her.

⅓ cup mealworms
2 medium cloves garlic, finely chopped
1 teaspoon tomato paste
1 tablespoon olive oil
1 teaspoon lemon juice
1 teaspoon red wine vinegar
⅛ teaspoon pepper
8 to 10 slices fresh French bread
   (½-inch slices)
1 teaspoon fresh parsley, finely chopped

Place mealworms, a few at a time, in a large mortar with the garlic and the tomato paste. Use a pestle to mash the mixture until it is a smooth puree. (A blender may be used instead of the mortar and pestle.) Add the oil a few drops at a time, stirring constantly, until the mixture becomes thick and smooth.

Stir in the lemon juice, vinegar and pepper. Cut crusts off bread and quarter each slice. Under the broiler, brown the bread lightly on one side. While the bread is warm, spread the untoasted, soft side with the mixture. Arrange the bread on a baking sheet and bake in the oven at 400° for 10 minutes. Sprinkle with parsley and serve while still warm.

Cricket Rumaki

Rumaki is a tasty Hawaiian dish. We made it even better with the addition of crickets and introduced it coast to coast on the Johnny Carson Show.

1 cup Insect Marinade (see *Basics*)
18 cleaned crickets
1 can (6-ounce) whole water chestnuts
9 slices bacon (cut in half to make 18)
18 toothpicks

Cook bacon slightly. Wrap ½ slice of bacon around 1 cricket and 1 small water chestnut (or ½ large water chestnut). Hold together with a toothpick, making sure the cricket and water chestnut are pierced. Marinate the cricket bundles in the marinade for 3 to 4 hours, periodically spooning the sauce mixture over the bundles. Place the appetizers in a shallow pan or cookie sheet and broil several minutes on each side until bacon is brown. Serve hot.

Tillamook Tarts

The cheese gives these tarts so savory a flavor that even Oregonians will take up insect cookery.

Biscuit dough (use your favorite recipe for 1 dozen biscuits)

Filling:
½ cup Tillamook cheese, grated
¼ cup marinated artichokes, chopped
¼ cup garlic butter fried mealworms, chopped
  (see Garlic Butter Fried Insects in *Basics*)
¼ cup fresh parsley, minced

Roll or pat dough until it is about ⅛ inch thick. Cut it into 3-inch squares. Place in the center of each square one teaspoon of the filling. Moisten the corner of the dough with water. Fold up the corners and pinch together to make a tart shape. Bake the tarts at 425° for about 10 minutes.

Salted Garlic Mealworms

Using mealworms, follow recipe for Garlic Butter Fried Insects (see *Basics*), adding ½-1 teaspoon salt.

Cricket Crisps

Using crickets, follow recipe for Garlic Butter Fried Insects (see *Basics*), adding ½-1 teaspoon hickory-flavored salt.

Sautéed Bacon-Pepper Bees

Using bees, follow recipe for Garlic Butter Fried Insects (see *Basics*), adding ½-1 teaspoon bacon pepper.

The Intimate Party For 6

Cocktails for six can be an unmitigated disaster. A friend of ours recently reported to us that she had invited her husband's boss and wife and her parents over for drinks prior to a benefit dinner. Mrs. Boss and the Mother arrived in identical dresses, both of which they had bought in the full belief that they were "originals." After exchanging furtive glares the two women sank into hostile silence. All others present, aware of the tension, fell mute. It would have been a session of sullen guzzling had it not been for the fact that the enterprising hostess produced such mouth-watering things to nibble on and comment about that the uneasiness of the potential cat fight was instantly forgotten. We like to think she served Sautéed Bacon-Pepper Bees. Rumor has it, however, that she served chocolate-covered dill pickles. We recommend the next few recipes as icebreakers for small gatherings, regardless of the attire.

Menu

Indonesian Hoppers
Peppery Delight
Sautéed Bacon=Pepper Bees
Empress Barbara Tart

Indonesian Hoppers

Here's a spicy, nutty hors d'oeuvre reminiscent of rijsttafel.

1 cup soy sauce
18 toothpicks
18 cleaned crickets
18 salted peanuts
3 tablespoons peanut butter
9 slices bacon (cut in half to make 18)

Marinate cleaned crickets in soy sauce for 2 hours. Cook bacon slightly. Wrap ½ slice of bacon around 1 cricket, 1 peanut and ½ teaspoon of peanut butter. Secure with a toothpick. Place on cookie sheet and broil until bacon is brown. Serve hot.

Peppery Delight

Made into a thinner consistency by the addition of more milk, this spread can be converted into an exciting dip for crackers, potato chips, or vegetables.

1 package (8-ounce) cream cheese
1 cup cooked mealworms, minced
   (see Basic Cooked Insects in *Basics*)
3 tablespoons onion, minced
1 tablespoon milk
1 teaspoon horseradish, creamed
¼ teaspoon salt
1 teaspoon pepper
⅓ cup slivered almonds, toasted

Place almonds in a 300° oven for about 5 minutes or until slightly brown. Combine all ingredients except almonds until well blended. Heat in baking dish for 15 minutes at 350°. Place in a small fondue pot. Sprinkle with almonds. Spread on toasted pumpernickel.

Sautéed Bacon-Pepper Bees

Using bees, follow recipe for Garlic Butter Fried Insects (see *Basics*), adding ½-1 teaspoon bacon pepper.

Empress Barbara Tart

One of Barbara's favorite creations is this pastry which we regard as worthy of royal status.

Pastry:

¾ cup sifted flour
¼ cup bee flour (see Basic Insect Flour
   in *Basics*)
½ teaspoon salt
¼ pound butter
3 tablespoons heavy cream

Sift both flours and salt into a bowl; cut in butter with a pastry blender. Stir in the cream with a fork until a ball of dough can be easily formed. Wrap in waxed paper or foil and chill for 2 hours.

Filling:

½ cup marinated insects
   (see Insect Marinade in *Basics*)
1 teaspoon salt
Dash cayenne pepper
1 egg, beaten
4 tablespoons butter, melted
3 cloves garlic, minced
2 tablespoons cornstarch

Mix all ingredients together. Roll out dough extra thin and cut into 3-inch circles. Place a heaping teaspoon of filling in the center. Turn in opposite ends and roll up. Seal the edges well. Arrange on a baking sheet and bake in a preheated 400° oven for 15 minutes. Serve with hot mustard.

Brunch

Bloody Mary Brunch

We understand that George Jessel invented the Bloody Mary out of necessity one morning about a half century ago. Three cheers for old George! We have no idea who invented the idea of brunch; presumably it came along after Mr. Jessel's stroke of genius. Whoever invented brunch invented an international meal—*le brunch, der brunch,* and *la bruncha.* This combo of breakfast and lunch, conveniently timed for late sleepers yet scheduled early enough in the day to allow for tennis or sailing or whatever afterwards, is an ideal way of casual entertainment. Bloody Marys or Bloody Shames (the nonalcoholic equivalent) are commonly served with brunch.

Incidentally, we have heard that the ideal time to learn to drive on the Los Angeles freeway system is at eleven o'clock on Sunday morning. A friend tells us that at that hour the Jews are on the golf course, the Catholics and Protestants are mostly in church, and everybody else is at brunch.

27

Menu
Baked Apple*   Beetle Sausage
Eggs en Cocotte
John the Baptist Bread
Sweet Butter à l'Orange

*Use your favorite recipe.

Beetle Sausage

Here's a sausage you can make yourself. It is one of our best dishes.

2 eggs, beaten
1 tablespoon each water and flour, mixed
2 tablespoons green onion, minced
½ cup fresh spinach, chopped
¾ teaspoon salt
1 cup mealworms, finely chopped
3 tablespoons vegetable oil

Combine all ingredients except oil. Heat the oil in a skillet. Drop mixture in hot oil to form patties about 4 inches in diameter. Brown on both sides, adding more oil if necessary. Serve while hot.

Eggs en Cocotte

We guarantee this dish to satisfy the most discriminating connoisseur of savories.

8 eggs
½ cup light cream
1 teaspoon salt
¼ teaspoon pepper
2 tablespoons butter
1 medium onion, diced
¼ cup cleaned crickets
Parsley, snipped

Sauté crickets and onion in butter until onions are translucent. Mix eggs, cream, salt and pepper. Add to cricket-onion mixture. Pour into small bakers or ramekins and cook in 350° oven until eggs are thickened but still moist. Sprinkle with snipped parsley.

John The Baptist Bread

Everyone knows that John the Baptist sustained himself on locusts and wild honey. By way of remembrance we offer St. John the Baptist Bread. For convenience, we have substituted crickets for locusts.

2½ cups flour
½ cup honey
3½ teaspoons baking powder
1 teaspoon salt
3 tablespoons vegetable oil
1 cup milk
2 eggs
1 cup dry roasted crickets, finely chopped
    (see Dry Roasted Insects in *Basics*)

Grease and flour loaf pan (9 x 5 x 3 inches). Add all ingredients except insects to a large mixing bowl. Beat on medium speed for about ½ minute or until smooth. Add insects and stir until well mixed, then pour into pan. Bake at 350° 45 to 55 minutes or until a toothpick comes out clean when inserted into the middle. Slice while hot. Spread with Sweet Butter à l'Orange.

Sweet Butter à l'Orange

¼ pound sweet butter, softened
2 tablespoons grated orange rind
    (For an added touch, soak grated orange rind in your favorite cordial.)

Mix with fork, place in serving dish, and refrigerate.

Champagne Brunch

An alternate brunch menu for more formal occasions is our Champagne Brunch. To us the words "Champagne," "bubbly," and "festive" are interchangeable. For those followers of Carrie Nation, Frances Willard, and Mrs. Rutherford B. Hayes, we recommend you serve your favorite sparkling soda garnished with a sprig of mint.

Menu

Peach, Grape, Strawberry Compote *
Cricket Patties Claremont
Honey Bee Soufflé
Stollen

*Use your favorite recipe.

Cricket Patties Claremont

Since we both live in Claremont, California, we presume it to be the insect cooking capital of the United States; we therefore decided to give recognition to the city by naming this savory after it.

½ cup cooked crickets
   (see Basic Cooked Insects in *Basics*)
½ teaspoon salt
Dash of pepper
½ teaspoon dry mustard
1 teaspoon Worcestershire sauce
1 egg yolk
1 teaspoon mayonnaise
1 teaspoon parsley, minced
Flour
1 egg, lightly beaten
Sifted bread crumbs
Vegetable oil

Mix crickets, salt, pepper, mustard, Worcestershire sauce, egg yolk, mayonnaise, and parsley. Shape into 4 cakes, pressing hard so that ingredients will remain together. Add a little flour if necessary. Coat with flour, then with egg. Roll in bread crumbs. Fry in oil, turning to brown both sides.

Honey Bee Soufflé

Everyone loves a soufflé, but wait until your guests try this one!

½ cup butter
½ cup flour, sifted
1½ teaspoons salt
½ teaspoon paprika
Dash of hot pepper sauce
2 cups milk
½ pound sharp cheddar cheese, grated
8 eggs, separated
½ cup marinated bees, chopped
   (see Insect Marinade in *Basics*)

Melt butter in a double boiler over boiling water. Add flour, salt, paprika and pepper sauce. Mix well. Gradually stir in milk and cook, stirring constantly, until sauce thickens. Add cheese to sauce and stir the mixture until the cheese melts. Remove from the heat. Beat the egg yolks until lemon yellow and gradually stir into the cheese sauce. Beat the egg whites until stiff. Fold cheese sauce into egg whites. Layer the bottom of a 1-quart greased soufflé baker with chopped bees. Pour the mixture over the bees and bake at 475° for 10 minutes. Reduce the heat to 400° and bake for 25 minutes longer.

Stollen

Stollen is a rich bread traditionally baked in Germany for the Yuletide. Candied bees make this bread something special.

2 packages dry yeast
¼ cup warm water
1¼ cups milk, scalded and cooled
6 cups flour, sifted
1½ cups butter
¾ cup sugar
3 eggs, beaten
¾ teaspoon salt
¾ teaspoon lemon rind
2 tablespoons brandy
½ pound raisins
½ pound blanched almonds, chopped
½ cup candied bees
    (see Candied Insects in *Basics*)

Dissolve yeast in warm water (115°) and add milk. Add flour one cup at a time until you are able to form a ball that is not too dry or too sticky. Roll the dough in a lightly greased bowl, and turn oily side up. Allow to rise in a warm place until double in volume (about 1½ hours). While the dough is rising beat the butter until soft, then add sugar. Add beaten eggs to the butter and sugar mixture. Next add the salt, lemon rind, brandy, raisins, almonds and bees. Punch down the doubled dough and fold the mixture into the dough. Knead the dough until smooth and elastic, about 5 minutes. Turn into a bowl and allow to rise until double, about 30 minutes. Divide into 2 loaves and place in lightly greased loaf pans. Brush tops with melted butter. Allow the loaves to rise until double. Preheat oven to 350°. Bake loaves for about 45 minutes, or until toothpick pushed into middle comes out clean and loaves are brown.

Lunch

Formal Lunch

The formal lunch has been relegated largely to the blue-rinsed crowd who still wear hats and gloves and pearls to these events. Bless their hearts. It's wonderful to see people take time to relax and enjoy life in the middle of the day. Maybe we all would enjoy eating well and ceremoniously at midday, enjoying food and conversation by daylight— something we seldom have time to do.

We especially encourage our readers to include men in the guest lists. Who knows, it might cut down on the tension factor in the macho existence.

We think the lunch we have suggested has flair. It is light, yet snappy, and lends itself to an imaginative table setting and perhaps a little Brahms or Schubert in the background. Because of the ingredients you might prefer not to serve it to your great-aunt Clarissa and her gang. On the other hand, why not? We find that veteran luncheoners of the old school are always interested in something new. This definitely is.

Menu

Cricket India

Insect Divan

Cold Artichokes with Lemon Butter *

Vanilla Ice Cream with

Jumping Jubilee

*Use your favorite recipe.

Cricket India

The spices in this appetizer give it a touch of India.

¾ cup garbanzo beans, dried
½ cup cleaned crickets, finely chopped
¾ cup onions, minced
½ tablespoon ginger root, minced
1 teaspoon pepper
1 teaspoon cumin, ground
1 teaspoon cinnamon
1 teaspoon cardamom
½ teaspoon mace
1 teaspoon salt
Juice from 2 lemons
3 eggs
½ cup flour
Vegetable oil for deep frying

Spread the garbanzo beans on a cookie sheet or in a shallow baking pan and bake at 350° for about 10 minutes. Cool and blend into a flour using an electric blender. Chop the crickets and add to them onion, spices and lemon juice. Mix well. Set this mixture aside for 30 minutes. In a second bowl, beat the eggs and blend in the garbanzo bean flour and the white flour until the mixture is smooth and thick. Add this to the insect mixture and blend the ingredients together. Form the mixture into "sticks" 2 inches long and ½ inch in diameter. (Add more flour if mixture is too sticky or water if too dry.) Fry until golden brown in oil heated to 365°. Serve as an appetizer either plain or with a cocktail sauce for dipping.

Insect Divan

This tasty entrée, although suggested for serving over rice, could easily be served over egg noodles.

¼ cup chives, chopped
4 tablespoons butter
¼ cup flour
2 cups milk
¼ cup water chestnuts, chopped
3 egg yolks
½ cup sherry
1 package frozen chopped broccoli
1 cup Basic Cooked Insects, chopped
   (see *Basics*)
Salt

Sauté the chives in butter. Strain melted butter into another pan and stir flour into butter. Add milk, water chestnuts, egg yolks, sherry, broccoli and chives. Stir vigorously over heat until sauce is thickened and smooth. Add insects, salt to taste, and serve over rice.

Jumping Jubilee

Brighten up the end of your meal by preparing this dish at the table.

½ cup preserved cherries, pitted
½ cup Candied Insects (see *Basics*)
¼ cup brandy, slightly warmed
2 tablespoons kirsch

Heat cherries and insects. When warm, add brandy. Flame the brandy. When the flame dies down, add kirsch. Serve over vanilla ice cream, or to be more traditional, serve over crêpes (see page 56).

California Lunch

California is known for its easy breezy existence, its casualness and its friendliness. It probably also has the best and most relaxed culinary style in the nation. Because Californians are "out-of-doors" types who thrive on activity, meals are often served simply and *al fresco*. The perfect complement to food is relaxation. This menu is a casual one which we suggest you serve on a low-key day, preferably outside. If you don't happen to live in California, we suggest that you pretend that you do while enjoying this lunch.

Menu

Cricket Louis

Rolls, Parsley Butter

Honey Bee Granola Bars

Cricket Louis*

Tired of Shrimp and Crab Louis? Then try our Cricket Louis. We think you'll come back for more.

1 cup cooked crickets, chilled
   (see Basic Cooked Insects in *Basics*)
Louis Dressing (below)
4 tomatoes, cut in quarters
4 hard-boiled eggs, cut in quarters
Ripe olives
4 cups lettuce leaves
6 ounces marinated artichoke hearts

Arrange lettuce leaves in a dish. Attractively arrange crickets, tomatoes, eggs, olives and artichokes on lettuce. Pour Louis Dressing over salad.

Louis Dressing

½ cup chili sauce
¾ cup mayonnaise
¼ cup green onion, chopped
¼ teaspoon Worcestershire sauce
½ teaspoon sugar
Salt to taste

Blend ingredients. Place in refrigerator until ready to serve.

*You may wish to substitute Chirping Stuffed Avocados here.

Chirping Stuffed Avocados

Here is a dish that can be served as either a salad or an entrée, depending on the occasion and your appetite.

4 ripened avocados
1 cup cooked crickets
   (see Basic Cooked Insects in *Basics*)
¾ cup catsup
¼ cup prepared horseradish
Juice of 1 lemon
Dash of pepper sauce
Head of lettuce

Cut avocados in half; remove pit. Combine crickets, catsup, horseradish, lemon juice and pepper sauce. Chill. Spoon into avocados and serve on a bed of lettuce.

Rolls

Use the Cricket-on-the-Hearth Bread recipe (see page 102) but place dough in muffin pans rather than the loaf pans. Cook at 350° for 10-15 minutes. Serve with Parsley Butter.

Parsley Butter

¼ pound butter, softened
3 tablespoons parsley, snipped

Combine with fork. Place in serving dish and refrigerate.

Honey Bee Granola Bars*

Our friends interested in natural foods should take to this snack.

4 cups rolled oats
¾ cups sunflower seeds
¾ cups coconut, shredded
½ cup sesame seeds
⅔ cup bee pollen
¾ cups slivered almonds
1 tablespoon cinnamon
1 cup honey
⅓ cup oil
¾ cup raisins

Mix dry ingredients, except raisins. Mix honey and oil. Combine wet and dry ingredients. Spread granola mixture over lightly greased cookie sheet. Bake at 325° for 35 minutes, stirring often for even baking. When partially cool, mix in ¾ cup raisins and then allow to cool completely. Cut into 3-inch squares.

*You may wish to substitute Beetle Bars or Popcorn Crunch instead.

Beetle Bars

A dish for the sweet tooth in your family.

1 cup granulated sugar
1 cup brown sugar, packed
⅔ cup milk
2 tablespoons corn syrup
⅛ teaspoon salt
2 tablespoons butter
1 teaspoon vanilla flavoring
½ cup dry roasted mealworms,
    finely chopped (see Dry Roasted
    Insects in *Basics*)

In a saucepan mix sugars, milk, corn syrup and salt. Cook over medium heat, stirring constantly until sugars are dissolved. Cook, stirring occasionally, until a small amount makes a ball when dropped into cold water or your candy thermometer reads 234°. Remove from heat and add butter. Cool mixture to 120°. Do not stir. Add vanilla; beat with a wooden spoon until mixture becomes thick and no longer glossy. Shape candy into 12-inch roll. Roll in ½ cup of finely chopped mealworms. Wrap in waxed paper. Chill until firm. Cut into ¼-inch slices.

Popcorn Crunch

Here's an easy treat to prepare and take to the drive-in movie. The kids will love it.

½ cup butter, melted
½ cup honey
3 quarts popcorn, popped
1 cup Dry Roasted Insects, chopped
  (see *Basics*)

Blend the butter and honey together in a saucepan and heat gently. Mix the popcorn with the insects and pour the butter-honey mixture over it. Mix well. Spread on a cookie sheet in a thin layer. Bake at 350° 10 to 15 minutes, or until crisp. Break into bite-sized pieces.

Dinner

French Dinner

Most people shudder at the thought of cooking and hosting a French dinner. The suggestion conjures up visions of endless hours over a hot stove creating and reducing sauces, elaborate table settings with all the stuff you wouldn't dare put in the dishwasher, and the use of linens which are impossible to launder. This is overreaction. A French dinner is different from others in one primary respect—it is served in courses, each of them rather spare in quantity so that at the end of the meal one has eaten well but not excessively. A French dinner needn't be an ordeal for the one who cooks and serves it. We serve our French dinners casually, sometimes on a bare table top. There's no need to put on the dog; after all, you'll be serving insects.

53

Menu

Insecte à l'Escargot

Soupe d'Asperges

Tarragon Crêpes

Haricots Verts avec Insectes

Tomates à la Provençale

Café Mousse

Insecte à l'Escargot

What's a French dinner without escargot? In our version we've substituted crickets for snails, and mushroom caps for the snail shells. The seasoning is essentially the same.

3 dozen cleaned crickets
1 cup Insect Broth (see *Basics*)
1 cup dry wine
3 cloves garlic, crushed
1 dozen mushroom caps, sautéed
    (see *Basics*)
Garlic Butter (see *Basics*)

Combine insects, broth, wine and garlic in a saucepan and bring to a boil. Cover and simmer for 1 hour. Uncover and reduce to 1 cup over high heat. Remove insects, saving broth for other recipes. Fill sautéed mushroom caps with several insects, depending on size. Coat with garlic butter and heat under broiler.

Soupe d'Asperges

Your guests will never know that their soup is fortified with insect protein unless you choose to tell them.

1 cup Insect Broth (see *Basics*)
1½ tablespoons cornstarch
Salt
1½ cups cooked asparagus, chopped
    into 2-inch pieces
1 egg, lightly beaten

Dilute broth to 4 cups. Dissolve cornstarch in 2 tablespoons of water and add to broth. Stir until mixture thickens and comes to a boil. Add salt to taste. Add asparagus to broth and when it reaches the boiling point again, add egg, allowing it to drip into the broth in a slow, steady stream. Stir and serve.

Tarragon Crêpes

We live today in the midst of a crêpes explosion, but we guarantee this version is different.

Filling

2 tablespoons butter
4 tablespoons flour
1 cup Insect Broth (see *Basics*)
½ teaspoon salt
⅛ teaspoon cayenne pepper
2 teaspoons dried tarragon
¼ cup Basic Cooked Insects (see *Basics*)
1 pound Sautéed Mushrooms, sliced
   (see *Basics*)
2 tablespoons dry sherry
1 cup heavy cream
Crêpes (see below)

Melt the butter in a saucepan. Add flour and stir until blended. Slowly stir in insect broth; add salt, cayenne and tarragon. Stir until smooth. Add insects and mushrooms. Continue to heat but do not boil. Add the sherry. Just before serving, add cream. Serve in patty shells or in crêpes.

Crêpes

½ cup all-purpose flour
¼ cup bee flour (see Basic Insect Flour
   in *Basics*)
½ teaspoon salt
2 eggs
⅔ cup milk
⅓ cup water
3 tablespoons butter, melted
Vegetable oil

Sift together the flours and salt. Beat the eggs and add the milk and water. Slowly combine the sifted ingredients and the liquid ingredients. Add melted butter. Ignore the lumps. Add a few drops of oil to a heated crêpe skillet. Add a small quantity of batter to the skillet and tip it until the batter covers the bottom. Cook over moderate heat. When the crêpe is brown, turn it over and brown the other side.

Haricots Verts Avec Insectes

Green beans are commonly garnished with almonds. Be different. Try our garlic butter fried mealworms instead.

6 quarts water
3 tablespoons salt
3 pounds green beans, trimmed
2 tablespoons butter
Salt
Pepper
½ cup garlic butter fried mealworms
   (see Garlic Butter Fried Insects in *Basics*)

In a large kettle, bring water and salt to a boil. Drop in beans. Return water to a boil, and boil beans uncovered for 15 minutes or until just tender. Drain. Melt butter in a saucepan and toss the beans with the butter. Season with salt and pepper. Transfer to a serving dish. Sprinkle with garlic butter fried mealworms before serving.

Tomates à la Provençale

Garnished with insects, a popular French vegetable becomes something special.

6 medium-sized firm, ripe tomatoes
1 cup bread crumbs
½ cup parsley, snipped
2 teaspoons dried basil, crumbled
1 large clove of garlic, crushed
1 teaspoon salt
¼ teaspoon pepper
½ cup garlic butter fried mealworms
    or crickets (see Garlic Butter Fried Insects
    in *Basics*)
⅓-½ cup olive oil

Cut the tomatoes in half crosswise and scoop out the pulp. In a large mixing bowl, combine the bread crumbs, parsley, basil, garlic, salt, pepper and insects. Add enough olive oil to moisten the mixture but still leave it crumbly. Fill each tomato half with the insect-crumb mixture, allowing the middle to be higher than the rest. Arrange the tomato halves in a lightly oiled baking dish. Bake at 375° for 20-30 minutes, or until tomatoes are tender.

Café Mousse

A rich dessert which includes one of the tastiest ways to prepare whole insects.

1 quart heavy cream, whipped
1¼ teaspoons coffee liqueur
½ cup sugar
4 tablespoons instant coffee
1 tablespoon gelatin dissolved in ¼ cup water
¼ cup candied bees
　(see Candied Insects in *Basics*)

Whip cream. Add coffee liqueur, sugar and coffee. Warm dissolved gelatin over low flame. Add gelatin to coffee mixture. Spoon into serving dishes, and sprinkle with candied bees. Freeze.

A Hearty Dinner

How to prepare a substantial meal for the family without spending an entire day in the kitchen is a problem for many women. Our hearty dinner involves minimum time over the stove with enough variety to satisfy the most discriminating taste and enough heartiness to satisfy your biggest eater.

61

Menu

Claremont Chowder

Spinach Salad

Maize Casserole

Tomates à la Provençale

Toffee

Claremont Chowder

Chowder no longer has to be an East Coast stew made with fish. We've named this unique insect chowder after a great western city—Claremont, California.

¼ cup bacon, diced
¼ cup onion, minced
1 cup Insect Broth* (see *Basics*)
2 cups peeled potatoes, diced
1 cup water
3 tablespoons butter
1 can (16-ounce) tomatoes
2 teaspoons parsley, snipped
1 teaspoon salt
⅛ teaspoon pepper

In a large saucepan, cook and stir bacon and onion over medium heat until bacon is crisp. Add insect broth, potatoes and water. Cook uncovered until potatoes are tender, about 10-15 minutes. Add butter, tomatoes, parsley and seasonings. Heat to boiling, stirring occasionally.

Spinach Salad

It's been an open secret for years among food lovers that spinach is really good. This nutritious salad is no exception.

1 pound spinach, washed
⅓ cup salad oil
¼ cup vinegar
¾ teaspoon salt
½ teaspoon pepper sauce
¼ teaspoon paprika
½ teaspoon dry mustard
1 clove garlic, crushed
3 hard-boiled eggs, chopped
¼ cup garlic butter fried mealworms
    (see Garlic Butter Fried Insects in *Basics*)

Tear spinach into bite-sized pieces in salad bowl and refrigerate. Combine oil, vinegar, seasonings and garlic and refrigerate for 1 hour. Toss dressing with spinach just before serving. Sprinkle with chopped eggs and mealworms.

*For more interesting chowder, prepare the broth as in *Basics,* but do not strain.

Maize Casserole*

We find that insects fit right in with this old-fashioned farmhouse dish.

3 cups fresh corn, cut from cob
    (approximately 4 ears)
1¼ cups soft bread crumbs
1 cup fresh insects
1 egg, beaten
1¼ teaspoons salt
1 tablespoon celery, chopped
⅛ teaspoon pepper
2 tablespoons onion, minced
4 tablespoons butter

Combine corn, ¼ cup of the crumbs, insects, egg, salt, celery, pepper, onion, and 2 tablespoons butter broken into small pieces. Turn the mixture into a greased, 1-quart casserole. Melt remaining butter, mix with remaining crumbs and sprinkle over top of casserole. Bake at 350° for 40 minutes or until crumbs are brown and corn is tender.

*You may want to use our Crickets and Mushrooms entrée or Cricket Pot Pie instead.

Crickets and Mushrooms

A very spicy dish, best when served over rice.

2 tablespoons butter
2 cups celery, finely chopped
¾ cup fresh mushrooms, sliced
½ cup small white onions
1 tablespoon soy sauce
1 teaspoon ginger
¼ teaspoon pepper
1 tablespoon cornstarch
1 tablespoon water
½ cup Insect Broth (see *Basics*)
1 cup cooked crickets
    (see Basic Cooked Insects in *Basics*)
2 cups hot cooked rice

In a large skillet, melt butter. Cook and stir celery, mushrooms, onions, soy sauce, ginger and pepper until celery is tender. Mix cornstarch and water. Stir cornstarch mixture and broth into vegetable mixture. Cook, stirring often, until mixture becomes thick. Stir in crickets. Heat. Spoon over rice.

Cricket Pot Pie

Don't be surprised if this dish is picked up by the manufacturers of frozen foods.

Pastry:
See *Basics*

Filling:
1½ cups Insect Broth
  (see *Basics*)
3 cups potatoes, diced
1 carrot, diced
1 large onion, finely chopped
2 tablespoons celery, finely chopped
1 cup cleaned crickets, finely chopped
⅛ teaspoon black pepper, freshly ground
¼ cup flour
½ cup light cream

Place insect broth, potatoes, carrot, onion and celery in a saucepan and bring mixture to a boil. Cover and simmer until vegetables are barely tender, about 10-12 minutes. Add crickets and pepper. Mix the flour with the cream and stir into cricket mixture. Bring to a boil, stirring until mixture thickens. Cool. Divide the pastry dough in half and roll out one half between sheets of wax paper to fit a deep 8-inch pie plate or casserole. Pour in cooked cricket mixture. Roll out remaining dough between sheets of wax paper and use to cover pie. Seal edges. Prick top of pie with fork. Bake at 400° for 10 minutes, reduce heat to 350° and bake until pastry is done, about 30 minutes.

Tomates à la Provençale

For recipe see page 58.

Toffee

Our first toffee recipe was done with the insects on the bottom of the pan. Most of our friends, however, prefer the insects incorporated into the mixture. Either way, this toffee makes an excellent snack-time treat.

¾ cup brown sugar, packed
½ cup butter
1 cup Dry Roasted Insects, coarsely chopped
   (see *Basics*)
½ cup semi-sweet chocolate, grated

Butter a baking pan (9 x 9 x 2 inches). Heat sugar and butter in a saucepan to boiling. Boil over medium heat for 7 minutes, stirring constantly. Remove from heat and stir in insects. Pour into pan. Sprinkle chocolate over hot mixture and cover so contained heat will melt chocolate. Spread the melted chocolate over the candy. While still warm, cut into 1½-inch squares. Refrigerate until firm.

Supper

Late evening suppers have long been a favorite for after the theater. These days you're just as likely to find us home watching the likes of Monday night football or Upstairs, Downstairs. Whatever the occasion, this supper will please.

Menu

Pizza Hopper

Jumping Melon Salad

Chocolate Chirpies

Pizza Hopper

You needn't wait until midnight to enjoy pizza. Next to hamburgers and hot dogs, pizza must be the runner-up for the all-American quick-meal favorite. Serve this to the guys when they monopolize the television set for football games.

Pizza Sauce

2 tablespoons olive oil
½ cup onion, finely chopped
1 tablespoon garlic, finely chopped
4 cups tomatoes, coarsely chopped but not
    drained
1 can (6-ounce) tomato paste
1 tablespoon dried oregano, crumbled
1 teaspoon basil
2 teaspoons sugar
1 teaspoon salt
Dash pepper

Cook onion in oil until tender. Add garlic and cook another 2 minutes, stirring constantly. Add tomatoes, tomato paste, oregano, basil, sugar, salt and pepper. Bring sauce to a boil and simmer uncovered for 1 hour. Stir occasionally. When completed, the sauce should be thick and smooth. Taste to see if more salt or pepper is needed.

Pizza Dough

1 package active dry yeast
2 tablespoons warm water (105 to 115°F)
1 teaspoon salt
Pinch of sugar
1 egg, well beaten
3 cups all-purpose flour
½ cup cornmeal
2 tablespoons olive oil
Pizza Sauce (see above)
1 pound mozzarella cheese, coarsely grated
1 cup dry roasted mealworms or crickets
    (see Dry Roasted Insects in *Basics*)

Dissolve yeast in warm water, and add salt, sugar, egg, flour, cornmeal and oil. Do not allow dough to rise. Turn onto well-floured cloth-covered board; knead for 2 or 3 minutes. Divide dough in half. Roll each half into 12-inch circle. Place on greased baking sheet. Punch up edges of circles. Spread one cup of pizza sauce on each pizza. Generously sprinkle with insects and cheese. Bake for 15 minutes at 400°.

Jumping Melon Salad

A delicious salad without the crickets, made even better with the crickets.

2 cups cooked crickets, finely chopped
   (see Basic Cooked Insects in *Basics*)
½ cup celery, diced
½ cup green pepper, chopped
¼ cup green onion, minced
1 teaspoon salt
⅓ cup mayonnaise
Salad greens
2 tomatoes, cut in quarters
8 melon wedges
Black olives (optional)

Combine crickets, celery, green pepper, green onion, salt and mayonnaise. Mix well. Arrange salad greens on large platter. Alternate melon wedges and tomato quarters. Spoon in cricket mixture. Garnish with black olives if desired. Chill and serve.

Chocolate Chirpies*

When Barbara discussed the eating of insects with a group of her 9th grade science students, they all wanted to know about "chocolate-covered ants." Here are our chocolate-covered insects, dedicated to her inquisitive students.

2 cups sugar
⅔ cup cream
2 ounces unsweetened chocolate
⅛ teaspoon salt
1 tablespoon butter
1 teaspoon vanilla
½ cup dry roasted crickets, chopped
    (see Dry Roasted Insects in *Basics*)

In a saucepan, mix sugar, cream, chocolate and salt. Cook over medium heat, stirring constantly until chocolate is melted and sugar is dissolved. Continue cooking, stirring occasionally, until candy thermometer reads 234° or until a small amount of mixture forms a ball when dropped into ice water. Remove mixture from heat and add butter.

Cool mixture to 120° without stirring. Add vanilla and beat vigorously with a wooden spoon until candy is thick and no longer glossy—about 7 to 10 minutes. Stir in insects. Spread evenly in a buttered loaf pan. Cool until firm. Cut into 2-inch squares.

*You may wish to use Banana Cicles instead.

Banana Cicles

Your kids will like them as much as Popsicles, and they're infinitely more nutritious.

¼ cup peanut butter
¼ cup powdered milk
1 tablespoon honey
⅓ cup light cream
4 bananas, peeled
⅓ cup Dry Roasted Insects, minced (see *Basics*)

Place peanut butter, powdered milk, honey and cream in an electric blender and blend until smooth. Roll the bananas in the mixture and sprinkle with insects. Freeze.

Celebrations

What follows is a list of celebrations for the whole year—off-beat celebrations which we provide as excuses for good times and parties. Every day is the anniversary of something and every day but one in the year is your un-birthday. We think that people ought to get together with their friends as often as possible, preferably to enjoy food together. It is our contention that you never need wait for a big occasion. Create occasions and spice them up with culinary exotica. What we offer here is to spur your imagination. A friend of ours always serves bugs on the anniversary of the Watergate break-in.

Chinese New Year

January 21 - February 19

This celebration is the biggest and most important festival of the Chinese year. The actual beginning of the festival is marked by the first new moon after the sun enters the sign of Aquarius. It is a time for trading the old for the new, a time when old accounts are settled. A farewell party is given for the old Kitchen God who will later make his report in heaven on the affairs of the household. Fireworks are exploded to chase away the evil spirits and prepare the way for the new Kitchen God who will arrive on New Year's Eve. On New Year's Day, a red scroll is placed on either door post to wish the household happiness, longevity and prosperity. As your contribution to détente, join the Chinese in their gala celebration and prepare the following menu for your favorite people.

Menu

Siu Mai   Egg Roll
Our Egg Drop Soup
Mealworm Chow Mein
Szechwan Supreme
Egg Foo Yung   Steamed Rice
Candied Insects
Fortune Cookies   Green Tea

Siu Mai

A friend of ours describes our Siu Mai as "bundles of gustatory excitement." We think you will agree.

1 cup mealworms
4 water chestnuts
4 tablespoons green onions, sliced
½ cup bamboo shoots, chopped
1 egg
1 teaspoon salt
1½ tablespoons soy sauce
2 tablespoons sherry
1 teaspoon sugar
1½ tablespoons cornstarch
¼ teaspoon pepper
Won ton wrappers
Dipping sauce (see below)
Vegetable oil

Place mealworms in blender, and grind until pastelike. Chop water chestnuts and add mealworm paste, green onions, bamboo shoots, egg, salt, soy sauce, sherry, sugar, cornstarch and pepper. Mix well. Fill center of won ton wrapper with 2 teaspoons of mixture. Fold won ton in shape of a triangle. Moisten finger tips, and seal edges. Fold creased corners backward and secure the ends with more water. (They should now be shaped as a bishop's cap.) Place in skillet containing oil heated to about 350°. Fry for about 5 minutes. Serve with Dipping Sauce.

Dipping Sauce:

1 teaspoon boiling water
1 teaspoon mustard
1 teaspoon vinegar
2 teaspoons soy sauce

Add boiling water to mustard and mix well. Add vinegar and soy sauce. Stir well.

Egg Roll

*Who ever thought a "bug in a rug" could be
so tasty?*

Egg roll skins (1 package)

Filling:

1 cup mealworms, chopped
4 green onions, chopped
1 tablespoon vegetable oil
½ cup bean sprouts, chopped
¼ cup water chestnuts, finely chopped
1 teaspoon fresh ginger root, grated
1 tablespoon soy sauce
Vegetable oil

Cook mealworms and onions in 1 tablespoon
oil for 4 minutes. Add other ingredients and
mix well. Place 1 tablespoon of filling in a
sausage shape along 1 side of a skin. Fold
over ends of skin and roll. Wet the edges of
the skin and press together. Fry in hot deep
fat at 375° for 8-10 minutes until skin is crisp
and brown. Cut each roll in 3 or 4 pieces
and serve.

Our Egg Drop Soup

*A chinese dinner always starts with a soup.
Ours is made with insect broth instead of
chicken broth.*

1 cup Insect Broth (see *Basics*)
2 cups water
1 egg
¼ cup chives

Dilute insect broth with water and heat to
just below boiling. Add the egg and stir
until the egg becomes stringy. Add the chives
and serve.

Mealworm Chow Mein

Mealworms make this chow mein distinctive.

1 cup celery, chopped
¼ cup onion, chopped
2 tablespoons green pepper, chopped
1 tablespoon butter
½ cup cooked mealworms, finely chopped
  (see Basic Cooked Insects in *Basics*)
½ cup chow mein noodles
1½ cups Insect Broth (see *Basics*)
½ cup light cream
⅛ teaspoon pepper

In a large skillet, cook and stir celery, onion and green pepper in the butter until onion is tender. Stir in mealworms, ¼ cup of the noodles, and the remaining ingredients. Pour into ungreased 1½-quart casserole. Sprinkle casserole with remaining chow mein noodles. Bake at 350°, uncovered, for 30 minutes.

Szechwan Supreme

A spicy Oriental dish we named after one of the largest provinces in China. A guest recently called it "supremely good."

2 cups Basic Cooked Insects (see *Basics*)
⅛ teaspoon salt
1 teaspoon Mirin (cooking sake)
⅛ teaspoon pepper
1 egg
½ teaspoon cornstarch
2 cups peanut oil
1 teaspoon chili paste with garlic
1 teaspoon fresh ginger, minced
1 cup Insect Broth (see *Basics*)
2 tablespoons soy sauce
1 tablespoon sugar
½ cup tomato sauce
2 tablespoons cornstarch, dissolved in
  6 tablespoons water
1 cup scallions, chopped
½ teaspoon peanut oil
½ teaspoon rice vinegar
2 cups hot cooked rice

Carefully mix together the insects, salt,
1 teaspoon sake, pepper and egg. Add the
undissolved cornstarch and mix again. Heat
2 cups of oil in a wok. When oil is hot but not
smoking, stir-fry insect mixture for about 15
seconds. Drain insect mixture, discarding the
oil. Clean the wok and mix in it the chili
paste, ginger, insect broth, soy sauce, sugar
and remaining sake. Put wok over high heat
until this bubbles. Add tomato sauce, insect
mixture, dissolved cornstarch, scallions,
½ teaspoon oil and vinegar. Stir-fry for 15
seconds. Reduce heat. Simmer for 10
minutes; remove from wok. Serve over rice.

Egg Foo Yung

*Disguised among the bean sprouts, you will
find our addition of mealworms. This is an
excellent dish to serve to those who would
like to try insects but feel they "just
couldn't." The bean sprouts and mealworms
both crunch and are indistinguishable. We
regard this creation as our pièce de résistance.*

2 tablespoons vegetable oil
1 medium green pepper, chopped
1 medium onion, chopped
½ cup cooked mealworms, chopped
   (see Basic Cooked Insects in *Basics*)
1 cup bean sprouts
1 can (8-ounce) water chestnuts, drained and
   thinly sliced
3 tablespoons soy sauce
5 eggs
Hot Soy Sauce (see below)

In a frying pan, heat 1 tablespoon of
vegetable oil. Add green pepper and onion
and cook until tender. Stir in mealworms,

bean sprouts, water chestnuts, and soy sauce. Heat thoroughly and remove from heat. In a bowl, beat eggs until thick. Stir in insect mixture. In a frying pan containing 1 tablespoon of heated vegetable oil, pour enough of the mixture to form small patties. Brown on each side. Serve warm with Hot Soy Sauce.

Hot Soy Sauce

2 cups beef bouillon*
2 tablespoons cornstarch
¼ cup water
2 tablespoons soy sauce

Heat bouillon to boiling. Blend cornstarch, water, and soy sauce. Stir gradually into bouillon. Cook, stirring constantly until mixture thickens and boils. Boil and stir for 1 minute.

*Insect Broth may be substituted for beef bouillon. See *Basics*.

Candied Insects

For recipe, see *Basics*.

A Mardi Gras Party

February 2 - March 9

Uninhibited merrymaking and hearty southern-style eating make the New Orleans Mardi Gras a most exuberant celebration. On your calendar, between February 2 and March 9, depending on Easter, you'll find Shrove Tuesday—it's the day before Ash Wednesday, the beginning of the Lenten fast. On this day of the last fling, this "fat Tuesday" (that's Mardi Gras in English), why not stage a marvelous, frivolous costume party climaxing in an original "down South" dinner featuring crickets that chirp among the magnolias and other delightful insect surprises from creole country.

Menu

Mother's Soup

Hot Cricket=Avocado Delight

Creole Pilaf

New Orleans Surprise Pie

Mother's Soup

A hearty robust soup which includes one of the favorite vegetables of the South—okra. This recipe was inspired by "cockroach broth" used by some mothers of the "Old South." It may not cure all your ills, but it will satisfy your taste buds.

½ cup shrimp, uncooked
¼ cup butter
1 pound okra, sliced
2 onions, chopped
1½ tablespoons Insect Flour (see *Basics*)
1 cup tomatoes
2 teaspoons salt
2 cloves garlic, crushed
Pepper sauce and Worcestershire sauce
   to taste
1 quart Insect Broth (see *Basics*)

Sauté shrimp in butter until pink. Remove shrimp and shell. Save butter and sauté okra and onions in it. Add insect flour to this mixture and thicken. Add remaining ingredients, including insect broth. Cook slowly at least 1 hour. Add shrimp before serving.

Hot Cricket-Avocado Delight

A hot salad that's just jumping with flavor.

1 cup cooked crickets, chopped
   (see Basic Cooked Insects in *Basics*)
⅓ cup celery, chopped
3 hard-boiled eggs
2 tablespoons pimiento, chopped
1 tablespoon onion, chopped
½ teaspoon salt
½ cup mayonnaise
4 small ripe avocados
Lemon juice
Salt
3 tablespoons dry bread crumbs
1 teaspoon butter, melted
2 tablespoons blanched, slivered almonds

Mix crickets, celery, eggs, pimiento, onion, ½ teaspoon salt, and mayonnaise. Cut unpeeled avocados lengthwise in half and remove the pits. Brush halves with lemon juice and sprinkle lightly with salt. Fill avocado halves with cricket mixture. Toss bread crumbs in butter and spoon over cricket mixture. Place in lightly greased shallow baking dish. Bake uncovered at 400° for 10 minutes. Sprinkle almonds over crumb topping; bake 5 minutes longer or until bubbly.

Creole Pilaf

Inspired by a French Quarter dish with all of the flair of New Orleans cookery.

1½ cups onions, chopped
1 cup celery, finely chopped
1 large green pepper, finely chopped
½ cup mushrooms, sliced
3 cloves garlic, finely chopped
¼ cup butter
1 can (15-ounce) tomato sauce
2 cups water
1 tablespoon dry sherry
2 teaspoons parsley, snipped
1 teaspoon salt
⅛ teaspoon red pepper
2 bay leaves, crushed
1 cup cleaned crickets
3 cups hot, cooked rice

In a medium-sized fry pan, combine the onion, celery, green pepper, mushrooms and garlic in butter. Cook until onion is tender. Remove from the heat and stir in tomato sauce, water, sherry and seasonings. Simmer uncovered for 10 minutes. Add crickets and stir. Heat to boiling. Cover and cook over low heat, stirring occasionally, for 1 hour or until crickets are tender. Serve over hot rice.

New Orleans Surprise Pie

Pecan pie is a Southern favorite. Here we have replaced the pecans with insects, and the result is wonderfully surprising.

Pastry (see *Basics*)

Filling

¼ cup butter
⅔ cup brown sugar, packed
2 eggs
¾ cup dark corn syrup
¼ teaspoon salt
1 teaspoon vanilla flavoring
¾ cup cleaned insects

Combine all ingredients except insects, and beat until smooth. Stir in insects. Pour into pastry-lined pie pan. Bake at 375° for 40 to 50 minutes or until set and pastry is nicely browned. Cool. Serve topped with whipped cream.

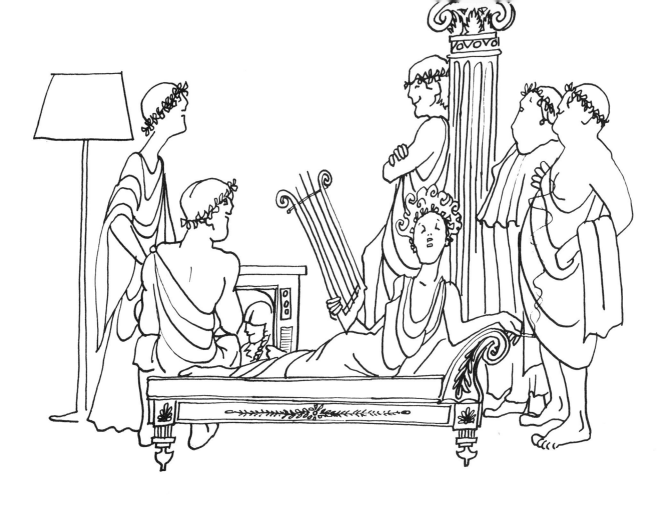

Birthday of Rome

April 21

This day celebrates the founding of the city of Rome in 753 B.C. Romulus and his twin brother, Remus, led the enslaved Latin settlers in rebellion against the Etruscans. Earlier they made a sensational food breakthrough by drinking wolf's milk. We suggest you celebrate both these occasions with an Italian dinner using insects.

89

Menu

Minestrone

Insalata Verde *

Polpette alla Salsa di Pomodori

Melanzane Italiano

Dolce alla Sicilia

*Use your favorite recipe.

Minestrone

A close Italian friend gave us this recipe (minus the insects), which his uncle serves at their family gatherings. He said that it is best when it can be simmered for an entire day. Being typical Americans, in a hurry, we cut the time and found it was still a scrumptious soup. Don't forget the Pesto.

1 cup mealworms
10 cups water
½ cup green split peas, washed
¼ cup whole barley, washed
¼ cup lentils, washed
1½ tablespoons salt
4 carrots, sliced
2 stalks celery, diced
1 medium onion, sliced
2 white turnips, diced in ¼-inch pieces
1 bay leaf, crumbled
Dash of thyme
Pesto (see below)
¼ cup chives

To the water, add mealworms, split peas, barley, lentils, salt, carrots, celery, onion, turnips, bay leaf, and thyme. Bring to a boil, then cover and simmer for 2 hours or until barley is tender. Put 1 spoonful of Pesto in each bowl just before serving, and garnish with chives.

Pesto

2 cups cilantro, coarsely chopped
2 tablespoons dried basil leaves
1 teaspoon salt
½ teaspoon pepper
2 teaspoons garlic, finely chopped
1 cup olive oil
½ cup Parmesan cheese, freshly grated

Combine cilantro, basil, salt, pepper, garlic, and olive oil in blender. Blend at high speed until the ingredients are smooth. The sauce should be thin enough to run off the spatula easily. If it seems too thick, blend in more olive oil. Transfer the sauce to a bowl and mix in the grated cheese.

Polpette Alla Salsa Di Pomodori

Polpette are an old friend, meatballs. Here they are made with mealworms. As a variation on this recipe, try it with your favorite pasta.

Sauce:

¼ cup peanut oil
2 cups onions, chopped
2 cloves garlic, minced
1 pound tomatoes, finely chopped
1 can (6-ounce) tomato paste
1½ teaspoons salt
½ teaspoon pepper
1 tablespoon basil

Heat the oil in a saucepan. Sauté the onions and garlic for 10 minutes. Add tomatoes, tomato paste, and seasonings. Bring mixture to a boil, then cook over low heat for 30 minutes.

Tenebrio Balls:

1 egg, beaten
2 cloves garlic, minced
2 tablespoons onion, minced
1 teaspoon salt
⅛ teaspoon red pepper
6 tablespoons cornstarch
1 cup mealworms, finely ground in blender
Vegetable oil
Flour

Combine eggs, garlic, onion, salt, pepper and cornstarch. Add ground mealworms to mixture and mix until smooth and fluffy. Flour your hands. Shape mixture into 1-inch balls. Heat oil to 375° and fry a few balls at a time until golden brown. Drain and add to sauce (see above). Cook over low heat for 20 minutes.

Melanzane Italiano

We recently served this dish at a small dinner party. All went well even after one lady asked for the recipe.

2 two-pound eggplants
½ pound butter
½ cup onions, minced
2 cloves garlic, minced
4 tablespoons celery, minced
2 cups insects, cleaned and chopped
2 cups soft bread crumbs
½ cup parsley, minced
1 teaspoon thyme
Salt

Wash and dry the eggplants, and cut them in half lengthwise. Scoop out the pulp, leaving a shell about ⅓ inch thick. Reserve shells. Chop the pulp. Melt the butter in a skillet; sauté the eggplant pulp, onions, garlic, and celery 10 minutes, stirring frequently. Mix the insects with the bread crumbs, parsley and thyme, then add the eggplant mixture. Mix gently but thoroughly, and salt to taste. Spoon into the shells and place on a greased baking pan. Bake at 375° for 30 minutes.

Dolce Alla Sicilia

A layer pound cake that can be sliced and served as a finger pastry or eaten with a fork.

A loaf-shaped Pound Cake (see page 95)
1 pound ricotta cheese
2 tablespoons cream
½ cup sugar
4 tablespoons Strega
4 tablespoons Candied Insects (see *Basics*)
4 ounces chocolate chips

Slice pound cake in 3 layers. Combine ricotta, cream, sugar, Strega, candied insects, and chocolate chips. Spread this mixture between the layers of pound cake. The top layer should be cake. Cover entire cake with your favorite chocolate icing. Chill for at least a day before serving.

Pound Cake

1¾ cups all-purpose flour
¼ cup mealworm flour
    (see Basic Insect Flour in *Basics*)
½ teaspoon salt
2 teaspoons baking powder
¾ cups butter
1½ cups sugar
5 eggs
1 teaspoon vanilla flavoring
½ cup milk

Sift flour before measuring. Add mealworm flour and resift. Add salt and baking powder. Resift. In a separate bowl, cream butter. Add sugar and continue creaming until mixture is light. Begin adding eggs, one at a time, beating after each addition. Add vanilla, then add the flour mixture alternately with the milk. Stir only until blended thoroughly. Bake for one hour at 325° in a greased and floured 4½ x 8-inch loaf pan.

Florentine Cricket Festival –a Picnic

In May

Ascension Day is a day of great festivity in many European countries. In Florence, Italy, families celebrate la Festa del Grillo, or Festival of the Cricket, for the cricket is the symbol of spring. A picnic is prepared and the families meet in the Cascino Public Gardens. Here vendors display crickets in brightly colored cages. The children take the crickets home and for those whose crickets are still singing when they arrive home, good luck is promised for the year.

We suggest you celebrate the Cricket Festival since it is the only celebration we can find anywhere in the world that has anything to do with insects.

Menu

Mung Bean Soup

Confetti Salad

Stuffed Cherry Tomatoes

Deviled Eggs   Insect Quiche

Cricket-on-the-Hearth Bread

Gravid Cookies

Bee-Oatmeal Cookies

Carob Fudge

Mung Bean Soup

A hearty soup, delicious anytime.

1 cup mung beans
6 cups insect broth (see *Basics*)
½ cup tomatoes, chopped
1 clove garlic, minced
1 onion, diced
1 teaspoon oil
½ teaspoon lemon rind
1 tablespoon lemon juice
2 tablespoons Dry Roasted Insects
    (see *Basics*)

Soak mung beans for at least 2 hours. Remove the skins and combine with all ingredients except the insects. Bring to gentle boil, cover and simmer 40 minutes. Spoon into bowls and garnish with dry roasted insects.

Confetti Salad

With colors of red, white, and green, this is a happy salad, almost too pretty to eat.

1 cup cooked crickets
    (see Basic Cooked Insects in *Basics*)
3 cups cooked rice
¼ cup celery, finely chopped
¼ cup pimiento-stuffed olives, finely chopped
¼ cup green peppers, chopped
¼ cup pimiento, chopped
¼ cup green onion, minced
½ teaspoon salt
¼ teaspoon pepper
3 tablespoons mayonnaise
1 tablespoon lemon juice
Lettuce
2 tomatoes, cut in wedges
½ cup French dressing

In a large bowl, combine crickets, rice, celery, olives, green pepper, pimiento and onion.

Cover and chill. Just before serving, mix salt, pepper and mayonnaise in a smaller bowl. Toss with cricket mixture. Add lemon juice and mix again. Spoon mixture on lettuce and garnish with tomato wedges. Serve with French dressing.

Stuffed Cherry Tomatoes

For recipe, see page 16.

Deviled Eggs

A picnic wouldn't be a picnic without deviled eggs. Add a flair to yours by garnishing them with our garlic-flavored mealworms.

8 hard-boiled eggs
3 tablespoons onion juice
2 tablespoons sour cream
3 tablespoons sautéed garlic mealworms,
 chopped (see Garlic Butter Fried Insects in
 Basics)

Remove yolks from eggs and mash with onion juice and sour cream. Fill egg halves with mixture and garnish with chopped mealworms.

Insect Quiche

This recipe suggests a whole new dimension in quiche cooking. We're up front about the insects; they're not camouflaged.

Pastry (see *Basics*)
¼ pound bacon, sliced into 1-inch lengths
¼ cup insects, cleaned
¾ cup Swiss cheese, diced
⅓ cup green onions, chopped
5 eggs
2 cups cream
¾ teaspoon salt
⅛ teaspoon cayenne pepper
2 tablespoons parsley, snipped

Prepare pastry for a one-crust pie. Brush crust with egg white and prick shell well. Fry bacon and insects in heavy skillet until bacon is almost crisp and drain on absorbent towels. Sprinkle insects, bacon, cheese and onion in pie shell. Beat together the remaining ingredients and pour custard mixture into pie shell. Bake at 375° for 35-45 minutes or until the top is golden brown. Serve in wedges.

Cricket-on-the-Hearth Bread

When Ron first served this bread on the Mike Douglas Show, Petula Clark commented that it contained too much caraway seed. We have since modified the recipe and believe it to be one of our better creations.

1 package dry yeast
¼ cup warm water (115°)
2 tablespoons sugar
1 tablespoon dry onion
1 tablespoon butter
⅓ teaspoon dill seed
⅛ teaspoon caraway seed
⅓ teaspoon celery seed
1 teaspoon salt
¼ cup crickets, cleaned and finely chopped
    (see Basic Cooked Insects in *Basics*)
1 egg
¼ cup milk, scalded and cooled
2-2½ cups flour

Dissolve the yeast in warm water. Combine yeast and all ingredients except the flour. Add the flour a little at a time until the dough becomes workable. Knead the dough until smooth (about 5 minutes). Place about 1 teaspoon of oil in a large bowl. Roll the dough in the oil and turn the oily side up. Cover and let rise in a warm place (76°) until double in size. Punch down the dough and turn into small loaf pans. Let rise again. Brush with butter and bake at 350° for 35-45 minutes.

Gravid Cookies

Take a simple refrigerator cookie recipe, add a sweet insect filling and you have created a nutritious treat that will go well in a picnic basket for your next outing or on a silver tray for your next formal gathering.

½ cup shortening
½ cup butter
½ cup granulated sugar
½ cup brown sugar, packed
2 eggs
2¾ cups flour
½ teaspoon baking soda
1 teaspoon salt
Insect Filling (see below)

In a large bowl, mix shortening, butter, sugars and eggs. Stir in flour, baking soda, and salt. Shape dough into two rolls, about 1½ inches in diameter. Wrap in waxed paper or aluminum foil and chill until firm, at least 3 hours. Cut rolls into ⅛-inch slices. Place about ½ inch apart on ungreased cookie sheet. Spoon ½ teaspoon Insect Filling onto each slice. Top this slice with another slice. Bake at 400° for 8 to 10 minutes or until done.

Insect Filling:

1 cup raisins, chopped
½ cup granulated sugar
½ cup water
½ cup Basic Cooked Insects, chopped
   (see *Basics*)

Add raisins, sugar and water to a saucepan, and cook over low heat, stirring constantly, until thick, about 5 minutes. Remove from heat and stir in insects of your choice.

Bee-Oatmeal Cookies

Warm oatmeal cookies, fresh out of the oven, and a glass of milk were grandmother's remedy for the "blah's." Take granny's advice. Whip up a batch of these oatmeal cookies and put a "buzz" back into your life.

¾ cup soft butter
2 eggs
1 teaspoon vanilla
1¼ cups honey
¼ cup water
2½ cups all-purpose flour
1 cup bee flour (see Insect Flour in *Basics*)
½ teaspoon baking powder
1 teaspoon soda
1 teaspoon salt
1 teaspoon cinnamon
½ teaspoon cloves
2 cups rolled oats

With wire whip, cream butter, eggs and vanilla. Add honey and water. In a separate bowl, blend flours, baking powder, soda, salt and spices. Stir together, and add oats. Stir completely. Drop rounded teaspoonfuls 2 inches apart on a lightly greased baking sheet. Bake 8 to 10 minutes at 350°. Makes 6 to 7 dozen cookies.

Carob Fudge*

Here's a way to satisfy your family's sweet tooth and nutritional needs at the same time. They're easy to make, so why not make it a family affair.

1½ cups honey
⅔ cup milk
2 tablespoons butter
⅓ cup carob powder
1 teaspoon vanilla
⅓ cup Dry Roasted Insects, chopped
    (see *Basics*)

Place honey, milk, butter and carob powder in a heavy saucepan. Heat, stirring until mixture is well blended and then cook, without stirring, until candy thermometer reads 238° or the mixture forms a soft ball when a drop is placed in cold water. Cool to lukewarm (120°) and then beat until mixture loses its glossiness. Add the vanilla and insects. Pour into a greased 8 x 8-inch pan. When set, cut into 2-inch squares.

*You may want to try our Peanut Butter Squares instead.

Peanut Butter Squares

Into natural foods? Then you'll love this treat.

½ cup powdered milk
½ cup peanut butter
1 cup shredded unsweetened coconut
½ cup sunflower seed kernels
¼ cup honey
¼ cup water
2 tablespoons brewer's yeast
½ cup Dry Roasted Insects (see *Basics*)

Combine all ingredients in a large bowl and mix until mixture sticks together. Press into a flat buttered pan. Cut into squares and serve.

Indian
Independence Day

August 15

We are told that the word "posh" was coined in the days when India was under British rule, and colonialists on ships from England to India and back preferred to travel "port out" and "starboard home." P.O.S.H. was stamped on their luggage if they were able to afford such preferred staterooms. The days of old Reggie and his adventures in "Injah" are long passed. Thanks to Gandhi and others, India became its own place after 200 years of colonial domination. The anniversary is August 15—a hot day in most places. The menu we offer here takes it for granted that it is *pukka* to eat curry in the heat.

Menu

Punjab Broth

Bombay Curry

Insect Chapatis

Sliced Cucumber with Yogurt

Gherkins *   Chutney *

Orange Sherbet *

Spiced Tea *

*Use your favorite recipe.

Punjab Broth

We borrowed the name of an Indian state for this spicy broth.

Cricket Broth (see Insect Broth in *Basics*), garnished with a sprig of cilantro and sliver of carrot.

Bombay Curry

In the home of some of our Indian friends, we were served this elegant curry. With a slight modification, the addition of crickets, we adapted it to our own special tastes.

½ cup butter
1 cup onion, minced
½ teaspoon ground mace
1 pinch saffron
1 clove garlic, minced
2 tablespoons curry powder
3 tart apples, peeled and diced
¼ cup flour
½ teaspoon salt
½ teaspoon coriander
¼ teaspoon ginger
1 cup Sautéed Mushrooms (see *Basics*)
1½ cups Insect Broth (see *Basics*)
1 cup milk
1 cup cooked crickets (see Basic Cooked
   Insects in *Basics*)
2 teaspoons lemon juice
Insect Chapatis (see page 111)

Melt butter in a large saucepan. Cook and stir onion, mace, saffron, garlic, curry powder, and diced apples in butter until onion is tender. Blend in flour, salt, coriander and ginger. Add mushrooms. Cook over low heat, stirring constantly until mixture is smooth and bubbly. Remove from heat and stir in insect broth and milk. Heat to boiling, stirring constantly. Boil and stir for 1 minute. Stir in crickets and lemon juice; heat through. Serve over rice.

Insect Chapatis

Our version of a basic Indian bread.

1½ cups all-purpose flour
½ cup Insect Flour (see *Basics*)
1½ cups water
Dash of salt
Melted butter

Mix water with flours until a stiff dough is obtained. Add salt. Knead bread until smooth. Pinch off pieces of dough and mold into balls about the size of a walnut. Roll each ball in flour and place on flour-covered board. Flatten balls to approximately ¼ inch thick. Heat a large, ungreased fry pan. Place a flattened ball in the pan and fry for 2 minutes on each side. Remove the bread and apply a little melted butter on each side and fry until dark brown spots begin to appear.

Sliced Cucumber with Yogurt

Peel and slice cucumbers. Serve with dollop of yogurt.

Moon-Viewing Festival

Mid-September

For centuries, the Japanese have practiced greeting the mid-September moon, which they regard as the clearest and most beautiful of the year. Late in the afternoon, just before twilight, the housewife places a low table on the veranda or perhaps on the windowsill, where the full moon will shed its rays, and upon it spreads an offering to the moon. Rice balls are put on the tray together with a vase containing the "seven grasses of autumn," cooked vegetables, chestnuts, and fruits. When the moon rises, members of the family and guests sit near the table, admire the beauty of the moon, and enjoy some refreshments. We regard this custom as one of the most beautiful we've heard of, and suggest that you institute it in your family.

113

Menu

Udon Soup
Cricket Seaweed Salad
Tempura Cricket with Vegetables
Tofu with Bean Sprouts
Lichee Nuts, Mandarin Oranges
Green Tea

Udon Soup

This light soup subtly awakens your taste buds to the gustatory pleasures of the dishes to follow.

2 cups Insect Broth (see *Basics*)
2 cups water
½ teaspoon salt
½ cup Udon noodles
4 spinach leaves, washed and torn
Lemon peel.

Mix ingredients together, bring to a boil and allow to simmer for 15 minutes. Garnish with lemon peel.

Cricket Seaweed Salad

You have probably been wondering how to prepare a dish with crickets and seaweed. Here we tell you how, and the result is surprisingly delicious.

2 cucumbers
Salt
½ cup cooked crickets (see Basic Cooked Insects in *Basics*)
2 or 3 one-foot-long thin strips of wakame (Japanese seaweed)
Water
1 tablespoon sugar
¼ cup Japanese rice vinegar

Peel cucumbers and cut in half lengthwise. Remove seeds. Slice cucumbers thinly and sprinkle with salt. Set aside for 10 minutes. After 10 minutes, rinse cucumbers and squeeze out the excess water. Add crickets to cucumbers. Soak the wakame in water for 5 minutes. Cut or tear soft portion of wakame into one-inch lengths. Discard the core. Combine cucumbers, crickets, and wakame. Mix together sugar, ½ teaspoon salt, and the vinegar. Pour over cucumber mixture and chill in refrigerator an hour or longer.

Tempura Cricket with Vegetables

Tempura is a favorite Japanese way of preparing sea food and vegetables. It's one of our favorite ways to prepare insects.

Dipping Sauce:

½ cup brown sugar
½ cup white vinegar
3 tablespoons cooking sherry or sake (Mirin)
2 tablespoons soy sauce

Mix the ingredients together.

Tempura Batter:

2 eggs
15 tablespoons cold water
¾ cup flour

Mix ingredients and beat until frothy. Keep cold until ready to use.

½ cup cleaned crickets
¼ cup soy sauce
1 cup peanut oil
Vegetables: asparagus, green beans, spinach

Marinate crickets in soy sauce for 1 hour. Drop crickets into tempura batter. Fry in peanut oil until light brown. Serve hot with Dipping Sauce.

Follow the same procedure, excluding the marinating, for asparagus, green beans, and spinach.

Tofu with Bean Sprouts

This hearty dish is a mini-meal in itself.

4 to 6 fresh bean cakes
2 dried mushrooms, soaked in water for
   30 minutes
2 teaspoons bean sauce
1 teaspoon soy sauce
⅛ teaspoon sugar
½ teaspoon cornstarch
½ cup Insect Broth (see *Basics*)
2 teaspoons salad oil
1 cup Basic Cooked Insects (see *Basics*)
1 cup bean sprouts
1 can (5-ounce) sliced bamboo shoots,
   drained
Minced green onions

Cut bean cakes into ½ x 1 x 1-inch blocks and set aside. Rinse mushrooms, discard stems, and slice into thin strips. Mix bean sauce, soy sauce, sugar, cornstarch, and broth. Place oil in wok over high heat. Add insects. Sauté for 2 minutes, turning so that the insects cook through. Add mushrooms, bean sprouts, bamboo shoots, and bean cakes. Pour sauce mixture in the wok. Cook, stirring until liquid is slightly thickened and smooth. Serve hot, garnished with minced green onions.

Basic Cooked Insects

1 cup cleaned insects
2 cups water
1 teaspoon salt
2 dashes pepper
1 tablespoon butter
½ teaspoon sage
2 tablespoons onion, finely chopped

Place ingredients in a medium-sized saucepan. Bring to a boil and allow to simmer for 30 minutes or until tender.

Dry Roasted Insects

Spread fresh, frozen, and cleaned insects on paper towels on a cookie sheet. Bake at 200° for 1-2 hours until desired state of dryness is reached. Check state of dryness by attempting to crush insect with a spoon.

Basic Insect Flour

Dry roast insects (see preceding recipe) and blend in electric blender until a delicate flour is produced. The amount of flour resulting from a given quantity of dry roasted insects varies with the insect used. One cup of bees, for example, reduces to a smaller quantity of flour than does 1 cup of mealworms.

Pastry

For an 8-inch pie crust.

1¼ cups flour
¼ cup bee flour (see preceding recipe)
½ teaspoon salt
½ cup shortening
4 tablespoons water

Mix together flours and salt. Cut in shortening with a pastry blender. Sprinkle with water, a tablespoon at a time. Mix with a fork until flour is moistened. Mold dough into a ball. Place on a lightly floured board. Flatten and roll out to about ⅛ inch thick. Keep pastry circular and roll it about 1 inch larger than the inverted pie pan. Fold pastry in half and transfer to the pie pan. Unfold and ease pastry loosely into the pan. Be careful not to stretch. Trim pastry with scissors ½ inch from edge of pan. Fold pastry under edges of pan. Flute the edges. Hook points under pan rim. Fill and bake according to recipe being used.

Insect Broth

1 cup water
1 cup cleaned insects
1 teaspoon salt
2 dashes white pepper
1 stalk celery, diced
¼ teaspoon lemon juice
1 bay leaf
1 tablespoon butter
2 tablespoons onion, finely chopped
1 teaspoon parsley

Combine all of the ingredients in a saucepan and bring to a boil. Cover and simmer for 1 hour. Cool and strain through cheesecloth, squeezing firmly to express all the juices. Measure. If less than 1 cup, add enough water to bring to 1 cup. If more than 1 cup, boil down.

Insect Marinade

1 cup soy sauce
¼ cup sake
1 large clove garlic, crushed
1 dried red pepper, crushed
2 tablespoons fresh ginger root, grated

Combine all ingredients.

To marinate insects, place them in the sauce for several hours, or if in a hurry, simmer for 20 minutes and cool.

Garlic Butter Fried Insects

¼ cup butter
6 cloves garlic, crushed
1 cup cleaned insects*

Melt butter in fry pan. Reduce heat. Sauté garlic in butter for 5 minutes. Add insects. Continue sautéeing for 10-15 minutes, stirring occasionally.

*Mealworms are especially delicious prepared in this manner.

Candied Insects

¼ cup butter
⅔ cup brown sugar, packed
¾ cup dark corn syrup
1 cup cleaned insects

Mix butter, sugar, and syrup. Beat until smooth. Stir in insects. Place in baking dish in oven at 375° for 30 minutes. Cool

Sautéed Mushrooms

2 tablespoons butter
1 tablespoon oil
1 clove garlic, crushed
1 pound mushrooms

Heat butter, oil, and garlic in skillet. Add the mushrooms (without stems if only caps are desired), shaking the pan in order to coat the mushrooms. Continue cooking uncovered for 3-5 minutes over moderately high heat, stirring frequently.

Garlic Butter

¾ cup butter
2 tablespoons green onions, minced
2 cloves garlic, crushed
1 tablespoon parsley, minced
½ teaspoon salt
¼ teaspoon pepper

Cream butter; add remaining ingredients and mix.

Appendices

Appendix 1:
How To Obtain Insects

All of the delicious meals presented in this book require a supply of insects. So where are you going to get them? Should you purchase canned insects, collect your own from the wild, purchase live insects from a dealer, or rear your own? There are advantages and disadvantages to each of these alternatives, depending on your particular needs and circumstances. In this section we discuss each of them in turn so that you will be able to choose the one most appropriate for you.

Canned Insects

Until recently a variety of insect foods, most of them canned, were being imported into the United States. Although you may still find some on your grocer's shelf, they are disappearing rapidly and are not being replaced. Most of these prepared foods are unpleasant tasting—some worse than others—or, at best, insipid. In our opinion, their disappearance is no loss. It is unfortunate that there aren't tasty insect foods on the American market, for there easily could be. Insects, which are eaten widely throughout the world, can be delicious, and there are many of you who are adventurous and who would be willing to try them and incorporate them into your diet—perhaps as ingredients in this book's recipes or perhaps even in recipes of your own devising. But for the time being, canned insects are out, so you are left with the three following alternatives.

Collecting Insects

Many insects are sufficiently abundant in nature that a few hours or a day in the field can turn up enough for a meal, or at least a snack. However, because of the heavy use of pesticides on our cultivated fields, forests, grasslands, and marshes, one is advised to collect only in areas known to be free of such contamination, for DDT and other pesticides may accumulate in the insects, making them unhealthy for man.

Hunting parties could be formed including members of the whole family. Armed with a butterfly net and a collecting vessel such as a glass jar, the hunters can enter the forest, field, or stream minus the danger which attends hunting with a firearm. Besides acquiring fare for a tasty snack or meal, one can learn a great deal about the habits and biology of numerous species of animal life. Also collecting insects in the wild helps one to appreciate their potential usefulness in wilderness survival.

Many of you, however, are city people with little opportunity to get into the great outdoors, and others—though anxious for an insect meal—cannot afford the time necessary to collect sufficient quantities of insects. If either is true for you, then you will surely find one of the following two alternatives your best means of obtaining insects.

Purchasing Live Insects

The purchase of live insects from commercial dealers is the simplest, albeit costliest, way to obtain insects for food. The most readily available commercial insects are the mealworm (a beetle larva, *Tenebrio molitor*), the house or gray cricket (*Acheta domesticus*), and the honey bee (*Apis mellifera*). For this reason, most of the recipes in this book were designed around these three insects. Special permits are not required for their purchase or interstate shipment, although you should satisfy yourself that the insects you purchase are free from insecticide or other contaminants. Sources of these insects, as well as several others for the more adventurous among our readers, are presented below:

Mealworms

The mealworm is a beetle larva generally sold in pet shops as food for pets and in bait shops as fish

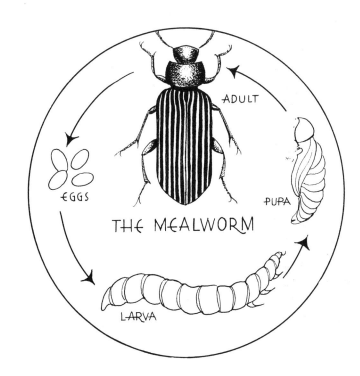

THE MEALWORM

EGGS

ADULT

PUPA

LARVA

bait. It is edible both as larvae and young pupae.
As a matter of fact, Turkish women are reported to
eat large quantities of mealworms in order to acquire
the plumpness their men admire so much.

You can purchase mealworms from your local pet
shop or bait shop if you wish, but you will pay less if
you buy from quantity dealers such as those listed
below:

Rainbow Bait Company
P.O. Box 4525
Compton, California   90224

Yarbrough Bait Distributors
Route 2, Box 202
Heidelberg, Mississippi   39439

Sure-Fire Fresh Bait
R. R. 6
Calgary, Alberta, Canada
(403) 273-9676

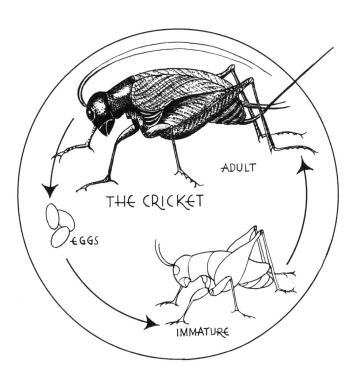

THE CRICKET

ADULT

EGGS

IMMATURE

Crickets

Crickets of all kinds are or have been eaten in many parts of the world. We are concerned here primarily with *Acheta domesticus,* the house or gray cricket. They are edible at all stages of their life cycle. Like the mealworms, crickets are often sold in pet shops and bait shops, and like the mealworms they will be less expensive if you buy them from a volume dealer such as those listed below:

Bait Unlimited, Inc.
Route 2, Box 10-A
Crawfordville, Georgia   30631
(404) 456-2830

Armstrong's Cricket Farm
P. O. Box 125
West Monroe, Louisiana   71291
(318) 325-2677

Yarbrough Bait Distributors
Route 2, Box 202
Heidelberg, Mississippi   39439

Selph's Cricket Ranch, Inc.
Box 2123
Memphis, Tennessee   38101
(901) 526-6896

Honey Bees

The larval, pupal, and adult stages of the honey bee have long been a favorite food of people around the world. Joseph Alsop wrote an article for the *Saturday Evening Post* entitled "My Adventures in Eating," which amounted to a four-star review of a Tokyo restaurant, the Akahane. A customary appetizer was fried bees, which, according to Alsop, achieved a flavor "halfway between pork cracklings and wild honey." Alsop stated that he really enjoyed them.

Although we used primarily the adult bees, in our opinion the brood, that is the larvae and pupae, are far tastier and more easily adapted to a wide variety of foods. They are, however, more difficult to obtain. If you want to obtain some, locate a beekeeper who specializes in removing wild swarms from locations where they are not wanted. Commonly these wild swarms contain honeycomb with brood which the beeman simply destroys. (See page 144 for suggestions on removing the brood from the honeycomb.)

Your best source of bees is a local beekeeper. You can simply consult the yellow pages of the telephone directory for the beekeeper nearest you.

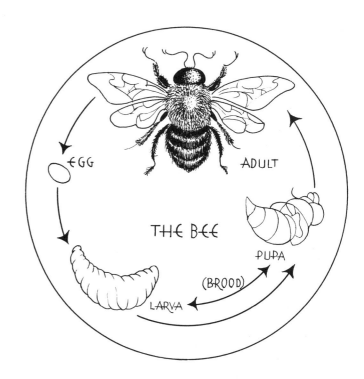

THE BEE

EGG   ADULT   PUPA   (BROOD)   LARVA

Fly Larvae

Flies have not been overlooked by humans as a source of food. The natives of some of the Oceanic Islands are said to prefer the maggots in their breadfruit to the breadfruit itself, and in Africa in the areas of Lakes Victoria and Nyasa, the lake fly is collected in great quantities and pressed together into sticky masses known as "Kungu Cakes," which are said to have a caviarlike flavor.

Unfortunately, commercial sources of flies are fairly uncommon. The flies that are reared are for bait and as hosts for parasites in biological control programs. Their purchase and interstate shipment may require special permits from either the United States Department of Agriculture or your equivalent state agency (or both). The supplier will let you know.

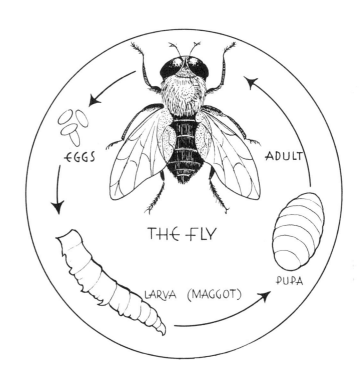

THE FLY

Insect Control and Research, Inc.
1330 Dillon Heights Avenue
Baltimore, Maryland   21228
(301) 747-4502

Sure-Fire Fresh Bait
R. R. 6
Calgary, Alberta, Canada
(403) 273-9676

Praying Mantises

Mantis eating has been reported from Papua, New Guinea, China, Japan, Thailand, and Africa. The praying mantis is a large insect which grows to a length of three to five inches. They are ferocious-looking creatures but they do not sting or bite and can become tame enough to be pets and to eat meat and insects from your fingers. Some species, when fried, reportedly taste like shrimp and raw mushrooms combined. Listed below is the only commercial source of praying mantises that we know of.

Beneficial Insect Company
555 Skyway
Paradise, California   95969

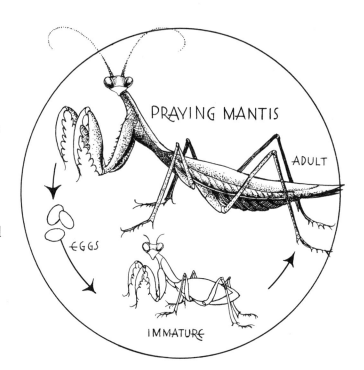

Rearing Your Own Insects

One advantage of insects is that their use allows you to rear your own animal protein at home. Obviously, someone living in a city apartment isn't going to maintain a cattle pen, a chicken coop, or a trout stream. Insects, however, require very little space, and since they neither moo, bleat, crow, nor cluck, there is little danger of disturbing the neighbors. The techniques for rearing the mealworm and cricket, two of the three insects which are featured in this book, are presented below. And should you be so ambitious, the techniques for rearing several other tasty insects are presented also.

Of course, many insects besides those discussed below can be reared and are suitable for human consumption: praying mantises, termites, and the immature stages of houseflies, for example. With a little knowledge of an insect's food habits and habitat requirements, the ingenious person can usually devise methods of rearing almost any type of insect. You might consult the entomology department of your state university or your nearest Agricultural Extension Service office for information on edible insects which you might rear and procedures for their rearing. They should at least be able to direct you to literature that would assist you in your endeavors.

Mealworms

Mealworms are best cultured in small pans or trays. Plastic dish pans are ideal, but shoe boxes or other similar-sized containers will work also. Fill the container with bran meal to a depth of two to four inches. Put about twenty-five to fifty adult mealworms into the pan, and place a small slice or two of potato or apple on top of the meal to provide needed moisture and an additional source of food. Maintenance of the culture will be simplified if the potato or apple is first peeled. Fresh potato or apple should be added every seven to ten days as needed. A thin layer of shredded paper should be laid over the top of the meal for the beetles to crawl on. The culture containers may be left uncovered because the beetles will be unable to crawl out. After three months, the culture should be checked regularly for adults and pupae. These should be removed to set up new cultures. More meal should be added as needed. If excess waste material (gray granular material) accumulates, it can be sifted out with a kitchen strainer.

The beetles start laying eggs seven to ten days after emergence and will lay between 400 to 500 eggs in a lifetime. The eggs hatch about fourteen days later into small white larvae. The time spent in the larval stage varies considerably with temperature and food availability. Under ideal conditions, the larvae grow rapidly until about one inch long, and then they pupate. The adults emerge two to three weeks after pupation and will live six months to a year in culture.

Crickets

The common black field cricket (*Acheta assimilis*) and the house cricket (*Acheta domesticus*), also known as the gray cricket, lend themselves readily to home production. Crickets for the initial colony may be bought from commercial suppliers, or they may be readily collected in the wild. Although nocturnal, the crickets may be found in the daytime around damp, cool places. Look under boards, rocks, dirt clods, or trash piles. Remember to avoid sources or places where insects may have been contaminated with insect sprays or other such material. From twenty to forty adult crickets should be used to stock each cage. At least half should be females, which are easily recognized by the lancelike structure that projects from the rear of the abdomen. This is the ovipositor with which the female inserts her eggs into the soil.

One-hundred-pound lard tins, sixteen by twenty inches, make excellent rearing cages. Place four inches of clean moist sand in the bottom of the cage, and put a handful of shredded newspaper on top of the sand as hiding and climbing places for the young crickets. Apply a thin coating of petroleum jelly to the top ten inches of the can so the crickets cannot crawl out, and place screen lids over the top of the cage to prevent adult crickets from jumping out.

Provide a glass jar drinking fountain of the type used for watering chickens (a one-pint jar inverted over a saucer would work fine). Place cotton in the exposed water to keep young crickets from drowning. Alternatively, slices of apple, pear, or potato can be provided for moisture. For feed, place poultry-laying mash or oatmeal in a shallow container (e.g., jar lid) on the floor of the cage. The water and food should be changed every week or two.

To encourage reproduction, the crickets should be reared at a temperature between 80° and 90°F. A sixty-watt bulb suspended in the cage may be

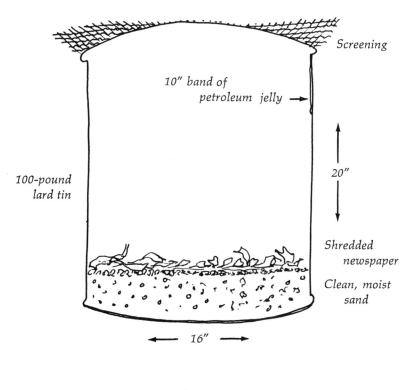

Screening

10" band of
petroleum jelly →

20"

100-pound
lard tin

Shredded
newspaper

Clean, moist
sand

← 16" →

Cricket cage

necessary to maintain warmth, but be careful not to overheat.

Some of the crickets will die, and these should be removed from the cages every few days.

The females will lay eggs in the moist sand, and baby crickets should appear twenty to twenty-five days after the cages are set up, and they will become mature adults approximately seventy-five days later. They mate within a few days after reaching maturity and the female cricket lays from 150 to 500 eggs over a period of one or two months.

Additional instructions for the rearing of crickets are contained in the following publications: (1) Anderson, L. D. and A. S. Deal (1972), *Rearing Crickets for Fish Bait and Other Uses,* One-sheet Answers No. 78, University of California Agricultural Extension Service, U. C. Riverside; (2) Sparks, L. M., *Raising Crickets for Bait,* Circular No. 464, Clemson Agricultural College, Clemson, South Carolina; and (3) Swingle, H. S. (1961), *Raising Crickets for Bait,* Leaflet No. 22, Alabama Polytechnic Institute, Agricultural Experiment Station, Auburn, Alabama. If additional assistance is required, your State Agricultural Extension Service could possibly help.

Most of the equipment necessary to rear crickets—the plans to build cricket cages, heaters for the cages, thermostats to control the heaters, thermometers, watering jars, special cricket feed, feed pans, excelsior, etc.—can be purchased from some of the cricket dealers. Both Armstrong's Cricket Farm and Selph's Cricket Ranch sell such supplies. (For addresses see page 127.)

Honey Bees

One who wishes to rear his own bees—not only for honey but for the larvae, pupae, and adults, all of which are edible—should get in touch with a local beekeeper and ask for his help and suggestions. You can also pick up a *Suburban Farm and Ranch Catalog* from Sears, Roebuck, and Co. or a *Farm and Garden Catalog* from Montgomery Ward, both of which contain sections on how to obtain information and supplies needed for bee raising. Raising bees is not only productive in terms of the food produced, but is also an educational enterprise that is enjoyed by many amateurs.

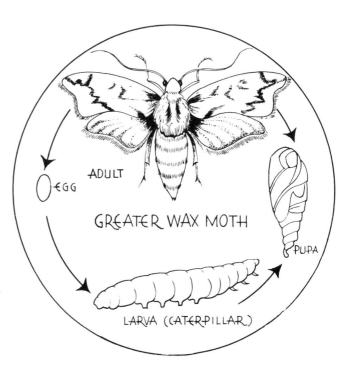

GREATER WAX MOTH

ADULT

EGG

PUPA

LARVA (CATERPILLAR)

Greater Wax Moth

Larvae of the greater wax moth (*Galleria mellonella*) are tasty and, fortunately, easily reared, hardy and odorless. If only they were commercially available, we would probably have centered most of our recipes around them. They are our favorite insect. They are thin-skinned, tender, and succulent. They would appear to lend themselves to commercial exploitation as snack items. When dropped into hot vegetable oil, the larvae immediately swell, elongate, and then burst. The resulting product looks nothing like an insect, but rather like popcorn. Anyone who enjoys the flavor of potato chips, corn puffs, or the like would delight in the taste of fried wax moth larvae. We can imagine them fried as above, salted, packaged in cellophane, and displayed in the supermarket alongside the other snack items.

About 1,000 eggs (see page 136) near hatching are placed in the bottom of a wide-mouthed gallon jar. To the eggs is added the medium necessary to rear the larvae to the cocooned stage. This medium is prepared by boiling together for several minutes one-third cup each of sugar, glycerol, and water. Cool and add one-fourth teaspoon of a vitamin mixture (Meads Deca-Vi-Sol), and five cups of dry Pablum (Mead-Johnson mixed cereal). Mix rapidly and place on top of the eggs in the rearing jar.

Cover each jar with a twenty mesh wire-screen disc, a paper towel and the jar lid, which should have a four-inch circular hole cut in the center. The purpose of the paper towel is to prevent foreign matter from entering the jar. Without the wire-screen, the larvae would eat through the paper and escape.

The culture jars are kept out of direct sunlight at 86°F for six weeks or 93°F (a very warm room) for four weeks to await cocooning. The moth survives well at temperatures ranging from 77°-99°F. When cocooning begins, mature larvae are harvested at three-day intervals from the inner walls of the culture jars without disturbing the medium. Removal after spinning begins insures that the insect has voided waste material. Mature cocooned larvae of good quality can be kept for over a year without pupating and with negligible losses by holding them at 59°F and 60 percent relative humidity.

By means of this rearing technique an average of 500 mature larvae weighing altogether some four to six ounces can be harvested from each jar. This represents an efficiency of food conversion of 20 to 30 percent.

To continue the colony it is necessary to rear some larvae to adults so that eggs may be collected. Place fifty cocooned larvae in a pint Mason jar. For egg deposition, add an accordion-folded piece of wax paper fastened with a paper clip. Cap the jar with paper towels held in place by the jar ring or a rubber band, and maintain at room temperature. Harvest the eggs about sixteen days after setting up the jar. A good yield is about 10,000 eggs per jar. Keep the eggs at room temperature, and you are ready to set up additional cultures.

The greater wax moth can be very damaging to bee hives, and for this reason they should not be allowed to escape from culture.

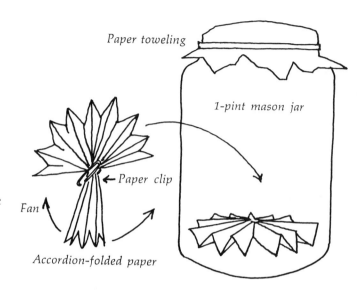

Wax moth rearing cage

Flour Beetles

Another easily reared insect, though much smaller and perhaps not as easily obtained, are the flour beetles (*Tribolium* spp.). These beetles are serious pests of stored grain, and so their shipment through the mails is carefully regulated by the United States Department of Agriculture. These (and other stored-grain pests) are not uncommonly found in the home pantry in flour that has not been used for a long period of time.

The beetles will thrive in a mixture of nineteen parts plain flour and one part dried yeast. Sift this mixture twice through a fine sieve, and place into a culture jar. Any glass jar—such as a baby food jar or even a small peanut butter jar—will work as a growing chamber. Close the jar with foam or cotton plugs and bake in an oven at 250°F for two hours. After cooling add twenty to twenty-five adults. At room temperature and approximately 70 percent humidity the beetles will develop from eggs to mature larvae and young pupae—the stages at which they should be harvested if they are to be used as human food—in four to six weeks. On the thirtieth day, and every day thereafter, the culture should be

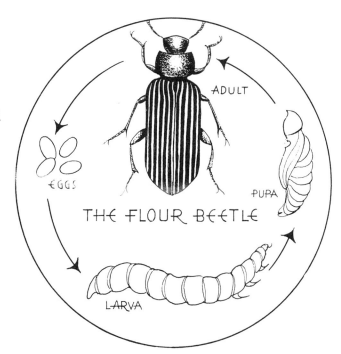

ADULT

EGGS

PUPA

THE FLOUR BEETLE

LARVA

examined and adult beetles removed because they are cannibalistic and will eat eggs, larvae, and pupae. If a faster life cycle is required or desired, the culture may be incubated at 90°F. At this temperature the life cycle requires twenty-three to twenty-five days. The insects are easily harvested by sifting the flour through a fine sieve such as a tea leaf strainer. The larvae and pupae can then be placed on a paper towel, and by gently blowing on them, cast skins and other debris will be readily removed, leaving only the clean, live insects for cooking.

Females begin egg-laying five to eight days after emergence. The larvae hatch in six to seven days, and the length of the maturation period depends upon the species, temperature, and relative humidity. The larvae pass through five to eleven stages of development, again depending on the species, temperature, and humidity. The pupal stage varies in length with the species and rearing conditions.

Blow Flies

Blow flies (*Sarcophaga* spp.) can be reared in a wire-screen cage measuring two feet on a side with an access door provided. Sugar should be placed in

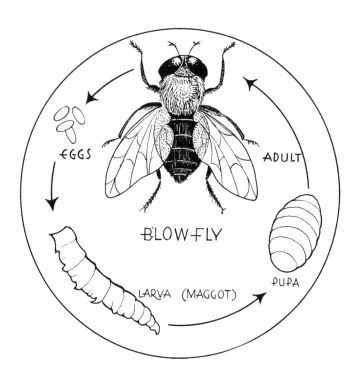

the cage in a shallow container, such as a jar lid. A shallow tray (about eight by twelve by two inches) with a one-half- to one-inch-deep bed of thoroughly wet wood shavings will provide a constant water source. Place a half pound of scored liver on the shavings in the tray for the flies to lay their eggs on. When the flies are laying well, the tray should be replaced daily with a new one containing fresh shavings and liver.

Larvae can be reared in a tray (about eighteen by ten by three inches) partially filled with three to three and one-half pounds of thinly sliced liver. The liver containing the freshly deposited eggs, as well as the water and wood shavings beneath it, should be spread over the surface of the fresh liver. Place this larval development tray in a large wooden box with openings at the bottom corners with jars attached. The box should be kept in a dark, humid room. The larvae will drop from the tray into the wooden box and migrate to the corners where they will fall into jars. They should be collected daily and frozen until there are sufficient numbers to process for food. Shoo-fly pie, anyone?

Appendix 2:
How To Clean and Prepare Insects

In this section, we pass on to you some helpful hints on how to clean and prepare insects for cooking. Once you begin working with the insects, you will develop your own procedures, some perhaps superior to those described here. We assume that most of our readers will purchase live insects through the mail, so we approach this discussion from that point of view. If, however, you either collect or rear your own insects, it will be a simple matter to adapt these instructions to your particular situation.

Insects, like lobster, are best if cooked while alive or fresh frozen. In contrast to beef, lamb, and poultry, postmortem changes rapidly render insects unpalatable. To facilitate meal planning, many species of insects may be kept alive for several days in the refrigerator. In fact, refrigeration before cooking is advised for the more active forms because it slows down their movements and facilitates handling. The experienced cook always tries to prevent the food from jumping out of the frying pan before it is properly cooked!

We generally use fresh frozen insects in our cooking. We prefer to order a sizable quantity of an insect, spend the necessary time to clean, package, and freeze them, and then always have them available for cooking on a moment's notice.

To those of you who are uninitiated in the procedures for cleaning and preparing insects for cooking, certain elements of the following discussion may seem unappetizing. We want to emphasize, however, that if you were to read instructions on how to kill and clean a steer or hog for cooking, you would surely find that discussion equally unappetizing. Unfortunately, you cannot purchase insects already prepared for cooking as is the case with beef, pork, chicken or lamb, for example. And it's worth noting that in dealing with insects the procedures in cleaning and preparation are on a much smaller scale than with larger animals. We certainly recognize that much of what follows will seem foreign to some, but in practice you'll find the procedures for cleaning and preparing insects simple and generally inoffensive. We present this discussion in considerable detail in order to give you as much assistance as possible and to give you the benefit of our experience. By all means, forge ahead. The result, a tasty meal, will be ample reward.

Mealworms

Depending on your dealer, mealworms will be packaged in either bran or crumpled newspaper. They will be active unless they have been kept under refrigeration. Their movements, however, are quite slow, and there is no risk of any of them getting away from you. Don't shy away from handling them directly.

Many people are more comfortable knowing that the intestinal tract of the mealworm they are about to eat is purged of all its contents or that it contains wholesome food. Well, in the first place, bran meal is a wholesome food, and we see little value in purging it from the mealworms or replacing it with any other food material. However, if your mealworms arrive in newspaper, then they have probably already emptied their gut of bran meal and replaced it with the only food available to them—newspaper—and you can easily eliminate the newspaper. This can be done by adding slices of apple, potato, or pear to the container and setting it aside for twenty-four hours. Given the choice between the newspaper and the fresh fruit or vegetable, the mealworms will choose the latter. The other alternative is to separate the mealworms completely from all food items for twenty-four hours, which gives them time to completely empty their gut. In the absence of anything to eat, however, the mealworms turn cannibalistic, and you run the risk of your prospective meal consuming itself.

As a first step in separating the mealworms from any attached food, waste material, or other debris, place a handful of them in a colander and gently toss. This process allows the smaller debris to pass through. By blowing on the mealworms as you toss them, the larger debris will blow out the top of the colander (just don't inhale the debris). You may find a blow dryer useful in this process. Now pour the mealworms onto waxed paper; the smooth surface prevents them from crawling too far.

The next step is to remove the dead mealworms. Death will occur during shipment due to cannibalism, rough handling, and, if packed in newspaper, perhaps starvation. The dead are easy to identify since they are generally darker in color and they are the ones that aren't moving. If you are in doubt as to whether a particular mealworm is alive or dead, simply touch it. You will know by its movements or the lack of them.

Any remaining cast skins or other debris that didn't pass through the colander are easily removed at this time by blowing on the insects.

The live mealworms are now placed in a colander and washed under cool water. We prefer to use a metal colander since the plastic ones do not drain as well. The mealworms are now placed on paper towels and patted dry. They are now ready for cooking or packaging and freezing for later use. We recommend packaging them in plastic sandwich bags in either one-half- or one-cup quantities. One cup of mealworms weighs approximately one-third of a pound.

Crickets

Your crickets will arrive packaged in a box containing newspaper or other material designed to provide as much surface area as possible for the crickets to cling to. They will not have been provided any food, so they will have begun to eat away at the packaging material. They will be famished and, depending on the length of time in transit, some will have died due to starvation. You should begin processing them immediately. Any delay now will mean more dead crickets, and you will simply complicate the cleaning process later and have fewer crickets to eat.

The crickets can be cleaned and processed immediately for consumption or purged as already described for mealworms. Use either slices of apple, potato, pear, or leafy vegetables, and set them aside at room temperature for approximately twenty-four hours.

Handling live crickets is very different from handling live mealworms. They jump, and unless you are careful, you'll have crickets all over your house. For this reason, we recommend that you leave them in the container they arrived in, and place them in your refrigerator for several hours until their movements are sluggish and they are easily handled. They cannot bite or sting you, so feel free to handle them directly. A word of caution, however: people with tender skin sometimes discover that the tiny spines on the legs of the crickets prick their fingers—perhaps not enough to draw blood, but enough to be uncomfortable. Such people should handle them more carefully.

Once the crickets' movements are sluggish, place a handful in a colander, and toss them while blowing vigorously into the colander; but, again, don't inhale the debris. The small debris will pass through the colander, and the light, larger debris will blow out the top. As we mentioned above when discussing the mealworms, you may find a blow dryer useful here. We find that lung power works better, but is also tiring if the shipment being cleaned is a large one.

Pour the crickets out on waxed paper and remove the dead ones. They will be darker than the live ones, and often their abdomens are shriveled. They may be difficult to recognize at first, but after a few minutes they will be easy to identify. Any remaining debris should be removed at this time.

Return the crickets to a clean colander and rinse in cool water, drain, place on paper towels, and pat dry. If the crickets are not to be prepared immediately for food, package them in plastic sandwich bags in either one-half- or one-cup quantities, and freeze them for later use.

If at any time during the preceding cleaning procedures the crickets become too active, simply return them to the refrigerator and slow them down again. To save time, they can be placed in a freezer.

Before the crickets are used in recipes, their legs and wings should be removed. We also remove the antennae and the ovipositor. Removal of heads is optional.

Removal of these various appendages is performed most easily after the crickets have been frozen solid or dry roasted. You decide which is better for you depending on the recipe you are preparing. The legs, ovipositor, and antennae are simply peeled off, the wings are pulled off, and the head is plucked off. Before removal of the appendages, one cup of crickets weighs approximately one-fifth of a pound.

Honey Bees

Adults. Bees are one of the easiest of all insects to clean, regardless of whether you keep your own hives, capture your own wild swarms, or purchase your bees either by mail, directly from a beekeeper, or from someone who specializes in removing wild swarms from areas where they aren't wanted.

There is always the possibility of being stung while handling bees, so be sure you get and follow professional instructions from your supplier or local beekeeper in order to avoid this uncomfortable and, if you are allergic, dangerous event. Following directions from your supplier, freeze the bees to kill them, then place a cupful in a colander. There will be virtually no foreign material unless the bees were taken from the wild, and then there may be only a few bits of honeycomb and some foliage. These are usually large enough to be picked out.

Wash the bees in cold water. *Do not use warm or hot water.* We learned the hard way that fresh frozen bees—even though dead—can sting while being washed in hot water. Keep your hands out of direct contact with the bees, and avoid being stung.

Allow the bees to drain, and pour out on paper towels. The bees hold a great deal of water and so must be thoroughly patted dry.

The bees are now ready for cooking or packaging and freezing. We package them in one-cup quantities in plastic sandwich bags. One cup of bees weighs approximately one-fifth of a pound.

Brood. The larvae and pupae of bees are collectively referred to as bee brood. The simplest way to get the brood out of the honeycomb is to put the comb in a kettle of water and heat on the stove until the wax completely melts. If you let the kettle cool, the wax will solidify on the surface and can be easily removed. The cooked brood will be found on the bottom of the kettle. You can eat them directly, incorporate them in various recipes, or freeze them for later use. One cup weighs approximately one-third of a pound.

Fly Larvae

We have to fudge a little here since we haven't experimented with fly larvae (maggots) in our cooking. Not because we are opposed to them, but because we haven't taken the time to rear them, and the only commercial sources we have found are outside California—one in Canada and one in Maryland (see page 138). Fly larvae are very perishable and do not survive shipment well if unrefrigerated for more than twenty-four hours. They are on our list of insects to try, and we will get around to them someday soon. We discuss fly larvae here because we know that the more adventurous among you would like either to rear your own or purchase them from commercial dealers.

Unfortunately, since we do not know how the commercial sources package fly larvae, we cannot tell you how to clean them. If you rear them as decribed on page 139, you would merely pour them from the glass jars into a sieve, rinse them, and freeze them until you have enough for a meal.

Fly larvae can be easily reared on clean material under controlled conditions. Purging wouldn't be necessary, but could be accomplished if desired by removing the larvae from their food source for twenty-four hours.

Although they would probably be good to eat in any form, they would appear to be particularly suited to drying and grinding into a flour that could be used to fortify breads, pastries, cakes, and other flour-based foods.

Appendix 3: Earthworm Cookery

As we pointed out earlier, although most people use the term *insects* to refer to all sorts of creatures, it really applies only to a particular animal group—the six-legged arthropods. Earthworms are legless, and therefore are not insects. They are scientifically classified under the major animal group known as the annelids, or segmented worms.

Because earthworms have received considerable attention in the press recently as an excellent and potentially economical source of human food, we have decided to include them here. From all accounts, they are a nutritious addition to human diets. And, importantly, they are 60 to 70 percent protein on a dry-weight basis. Among their advantages is that they are entirely edible, with no bone or gristle to throw away, and their subtle, earthy flavor lends itself well to all sorts of delightful dishes. We cook with earthworms and find them as palatable as many insects.

Recipes

Recently North American Bait Farms, Inc., of Ontario, California, sponsored an Earthworm Recipe Contest.

Using the French term for earthworm, which is *ver de terre,* the announcement for the contest called for dishes such as: Canapés Ver de Terre, Consommé Ver de Terre, Caesar Salade au Ver de Terre, Ver de Terre Bourguignon, Ver de Terre au Fromage Suisse, Ragout Ver de Terre, Ver de Terre Forestier, Ver de Terre au Champignons, Ver de Terre au Truffe, and Petit Gâteau au Ver de Terre.

One of us served as a judge at this contest, which was held at California State Polytechnic University, Pomona. Thanks to the courtesy of the contest's sponsors, we are pleased to present below the six recipe finalists.* The winning recipe was the Applesauce Surprise Cake.

*We have edited these recipes for consistency of style.

Earthworm Omelette

6 eggs
⅓ cup milk
¼ cup parsley
½ teaspoon seasoned salt
½ teaspoon pepper
1 drop garlic extract
¾ to 1 cup fresh earthworms
¼ cup celery, sliced
⅓ cup green pepper, sliced
¼ small onion, chopped
⅓ cup American cheese, shredded
⅓ cup mushrooms, sliced (optional)
1 drop hot pepper sauce
1 dash Worcestershire sauce

Beat together eggs, milk, parsley, salt, pepper, and garlic. Place mixture in a medium-hot omelette pan. When almost done to taste, add earthworms, celery, green pepper, onion, cheese and mushrooms. Finish cooking. Add pepper sauce and Worchestershire sauce. Serve immediately.

Submitted by: Robert J. Smith

Earthworm Patties Supreme

1½ pounds earthworms, ground
½ cup butter, melted
1 teaspoon lemon rind, grated
1½ teaspoons salt
½ teaspoon white pepper
2 tablespoons plain soda water (for lightness)
1 egg, beaten
1 cup dry bread crumbs
2 tablespoons butter
1 cup sour cream

Combine earthworms, melted butter, lemon rind, salt, and pepper. Stir in soda water. Shape into patties and dip in beaten egg, then bread crumbs. Place in heated butter and cook for 10 minutes, turning once. Place the patties on hot serving dish. Stir sour cream into skillet and heat thoroughly. Pour over patties. May be served with plain boiled potatoes.

Submitted by: Patricia H. Howell

Ver de Terre in Deviled Shrimp Hors d'Oeuvres

1 cup earthworms
¾ cup blanched almonds
6 hard-boiled eggs
2 to 4 tablespoons mayonnaise
1 can cocktail shrimp, drained and rinsed
½ cup celery, finely chopped
¾ cup cheddar cheese, grated
⅛ teaspoon onion salt
⅛ teaspoon garlic salt
⅛ teaspoon salt
1 loaf sourdough bread, sliced

Wash earthworms and boil for 15 minutes.
Rinse and repeat boiling; rinse and pat dry.
Chop almonds and mix with earthworms.
Spread mixture on cookie sheet and toast in a
hot oven. Mash together eggs, mayonnaise,
shrimp, celery and salts. Mix together
earthworms and egg-shrimp mixture. Spread
on sourdough squares. Bake at 350° for
15 minutes. Top with cheese and bake until
cheese melts.

Submitted by: Vicky Ash

Curried Ver de Terre and Pea Soufflé

1 cup milk
¾ cup fresh coconut, grated
½ teaspoon brown sugar
¼ cup butter
1 small onion, grated
1 clove garlic
1½ teaspoons curry powder
3 tablespoons flour
4 egg yolks
1 cup peas
1 cup earthworms, cut in ½-inch lengths
4 egg whites, beaten until stiff
Salt and pepper to taste

Curry Sauce:

Heat milk in a saucepan. Stir in coconut and brown sugar. Allow the mixture to cool. In the butter, sauté onion well. Add garlic and continue to cook. Stir in curry powder and gradually add the coconut mixture. Then add flour mixed to a paste in milk and cook for 5 minutes longer. Allow to cool slightly.

In another pan, beat the egg yolks. While stirring egg yolks, gradually add the curry sauce. Mix in peas and 1 cup of prepared earthworms. Fold in egg whites and season with salt and pepper. Turn mixture into a buttered soufflé dish and bake at 375° for 40 minutes.

Submitted by: George H. Lewis

Ver de Terre Stuffed Peppers

2¼ cups earthworms
½ pound lean hamburger
1 onion, chopped
1 clove garlic, minced
1 teaspoon parsley
⅛ teaspoon pepper
¼ teaspoon salt
2 cans (8-ounce) tomato sauce
1 large mushroom, thinly sliced
4 to 6 bell peppers
1 package long grain wild rice
¾ cup cheddar cheese, grated

Wash earthworms and boil for 15 minutes. Rinse and repeat boiling; rinse and pat dry. Fry together with hamburger, onions, garlic, parsley, pepper, salt, tomato sauce, and mushrooms. Boil bell peppers for 15 minutes, or until tender. Mix the rice with the hamburger-earthworm mixture. Stuff the peppers with the mixture and bake at 350° for 25 minutes. Top with grated cheese and bake for 5 minutes longer. Serve with chilled cream of avocado soup or carrot-raisin salad.

Submitted by: Vicky Ash

Applesauce Surprise Cake

1 cup dried earthworms, chopped (see below)
½ cup butter
1½ cups sugar
3 eggs
2 cups flour
1 teaspoon baking soda
1 teaspoon cinnamon
½ teaspoon salt
½ teaspoon nutmeg
½ teaspoon cloves
1½ cups applesauce
½ cup nuts, chopped

Chop earthworms and spread on a Teflon cookie sheet. Place in 200° oven for 15 minutes. Remove and let cool. Cream together butter, sugar and eggs. Sift dry ingredients together and add to the egg mixture. Add applesauce, earthworms, and nuts. Mix well. Pour into well-greased 10-inch tube pan or Bundt pan. Bake at 325° for 50 minutes.

Submitted by: Patricia H. Howell

Apart from the above contest, we have been provided with another recipe by Wilken's Worm Farm of Solano Beach, California:

Peanut Butter-Worm Cookies

½ pound earthworms
1 cup peanut butter
1 egg
1 cup sugar
1 cup flour
1 teaspoon vanilla

Boil the earthworms for 10 minutes and drain. Mix together all ingredients. Roll dough into small balls and place 1 inch apart on ungreased cookie sheet. Bake at 350° for 15 minutes.

The growing interest in this source of food was additionally attested to by an article in the San Francisco *Examiner* reporting a similar recipe contest held in that city. The entries included appetizers such as Paté de Chenilles Larves and St. Patrick Table-Bait Hors d'Oeuvres; hot dishes such as Earthworms Escargot, Earthworms Oriental, and Stuff-a-Wigglie-a-Roni; and desserts such as EEK!-Cology Cookies, Banana Raisin Eisenia Bread, and Ver et Noix Torte.

In the following pages we discuss commercial sources of earthworms, how to rear your own, and how to clean and prepare them for cooking.

Purchasing Live Earthworms

Although most earthworm dealers sell the familiar red worm or red wiggler, many of them also sell night crawlers, white worms, and various other species. Although all earthworms are presumably edible, the red worm is the only one we've had any experience with. Listed below are the dealers that have responded to our queries, although you will find many others listed in the *Earthworm Buyer's Guide*, Shields Publications, P. O. Box 472, Elgin, Illinois 60120. As with insects, earthworms can often be purchased in pet shops and bait shops, but you will have to pay premium prices. We recommend that you purchase from one of the bulk dealers. In any case, get sufficient information from your source of supply to satisfy yourself that your worms are free of insecticides or other contaminants.

Arizona Bait Farm
P.O. Box 458
Lakeside, Arizona   85929

J & M Bait Company
21310 Community Street
Canoga Park, California   91304

Bud Kinney Finest Red Worms
Route 1, Box 438-T
Chico, California   95926
(916) 342-5863

Longmire's Worm Farm
Star Route Etlersburg
Garberville, California   95440

Hy Hunter Industries
P. O. Box 3537
Granada Hills, California   91344
(213) 363-0202

Russian River Worm Farm
2161 West Dry Creek
Healdsburg, California   95448
(707) 433-5349

Earthworm Oasis, Inc.
40892 Harper Lake Road
Hinkley, California   92347
(714) 256-8574

North American Bait Farms, Inc.
1207 S. Palmetto
Ontario, California   91761

Red Wiggle Hollow
P.O. Box 1144
Dept. BG
San Gabriel, California   91778
(213) 285-6466

Wilken's Worm Farm
604 Canyon Place
Solano Beach, California   92075
(714) 755-1082

Bait Unlimited, Inc.
Route 2, Box 10-A
Crawfordville, Georgia   30631
(404) 456-2830

The Bait Barn Worm Farm
Route 1, Box 61K
Coeur d'Alene, Idaho   83814
(208) 664-9952

Earthland, Inc.
Box 166
Williamsport, Maryland   21795
(301) 223-8134

Hillaire Worm Farms
Box 249
Northville, Michigan   48167

Yarbrough Bait Distributors
Route 2, Box 202
Heidelberg, Mississippi   39439

Ozark Worm Farms
Willow Springs, Missouri   65793
(417) 469-2217

Monadnock Rabbitry and Worm Farm
Box 403
Troy, New Hampshire   03465
(603) 242-6668

Worm Ranch
408 Cole Road
Blackwood, New Jersey   08012
(609) 227-9345

Lucus Worm Farm
19708 N.E. 157th Avenue
Battleground, Washington   98604
(206) 687-4948

The Bait Barn Worm Farm
601 Old Tulalip Road West
Marysville, Washington   98270

Sure-Fire Fresh Bait
R. R. 6
Calgary, Alberta, Canada
(403) 273-9676

Rearing Your Own

Although we have not tried rearing earthworms ourselves, we are told by both professional and amateur earthworm farmers that rearing them is not only easy and inexpensive, but also fun. Numerous books are available on the techniques of rearing earthworms. One excellent book is by Ronald E. Gaddie, Sr., and Donald E. Douglas, entitled *Earthworms for Ecology and Profit,* published by North American Bait Farms, Inc., 1207 S. Palmetto, Ontario, California 91761 (Phone: 714-983-3676). North American Bait Farms is also a source of rearing supplies. Another important source for information about earthworm-rearing supplies is the *Earthworm Buyer's Guide,* published by Shields Publications, P.O. Box 472, Elgin, Illinois, 60120. This book, as well as *Earthworms for Ecology and Profit,* can probably be picked up at your local earthworm dealer, of which we are told there are over 10,000 in the United States.

A "Worm Culture Box" is sold by Wilken's Worm Farm, 604 Canyon Place, Solano Beach, California 92075 (Phone: 714-755-1082). They advertise that it can be used either indoors or outdoors, and that it will produce 40,000 worms annually. The kit includes 1,000 worms, culture box, lid, worm bedding, vitamins, walnut meal, medicine, instructions, and two clay pots with starting soil. (It apparently doubles as a planter.)

Earthworms will more than double their population every two months and will eat any decayed, organic material. By composting kitchen waste with redworms the consumer can do three things simultaneously: (1) recycle his organic refuse without the costly energy requirements for hauling it away; (2) manufacture one of the best fertilizers and soil conditioners (worm castings) known to man for use in his vegetable or flower garden; and (3) grow a usable animal protein for himself and his family that after an initial investment renews itself.

Under suitable conditions 1,000 earthworm breeders will become 1,000,000 breeders, babies, and egg capsules within a year. A breeder worm will produce three to four egg capsules each month. Each capsule in turn hatches two to twenty young, which grow to breeding size in from two to three months. Because they are bisexual, every worm is a breeder. The worms will live up to ten years—much less of course if you harvest them regularly and eat them.

How To Clean and Prepare Earthworms

Your earthworms will probably not require purging if you buy them from a dealer who packages them in peat moss for shipping. Earthworms eat and expel material equal to their weight every twenty-four hours, so the worms will have essentially only peat moss in their bodies. By the time you get them, any material they had been raised on would probably have been purged from their bodies. The small amounts of peat moss that one would be eating with the worms would be negligible. One might even rationalize that the additional roughage would be good for you anyway. For any further purging, place them in moist cornmeal, flour, or similar material for twenty-four hours. In this way, you can be certain that the worms will be clean inside and out and ready to cook.

Earthworms may be kept for a few days in the shipping material if kept under refrigeration or in a cool place. Temperatures above 60°F are harmful to earthworms. The shipping material should be kept moist. We recommend, however, that you clean your earthworms immediately after receiving them.

Place a handful of earthworms on waxed paper, and remove the dead ones. Look for true movement and not just movement caused by a live worm moving against a dead worm. After removal of the dead worms, place a handful of worms in a colander. Rinse vigorously with cold water. If handled too hesitantly they will crawl through the holes in the colander, complicating the process. Place on paper towels and pat dry. The worms are now ready to use in your recipes, or may be packaged and frozen for later use. We package them in one-half-cup quantities in plastic sandwich bags. One cup of earthworms weighs approximately one-half pound.

The rinsed worms are generally boiled before inclusion in any recipe. They may be boiled for as little as ten minutes, although some earthworm chefs will boil them as many as five separate times for ten minutes each time. They may then be incorporated directly into the recipes or they may be placed on a cookie sheet in a 200° oven for fifteen to thirty minutes. They may be used whole, chopped, or as a flour. The flour is most easily prepared by use of a blender.

Indices

Index of Recipes

Index of Appendices